A-LEVEL

STUDENT GUIDE

WJEC

History

Unit 4: Nazi Germany c.1933–45

Gareth Holt

HODDER
EDUCATION
AN HACHETTE UK COMPANY

Hodder Education, an Hachette Company, Carmelite House, 50 Victoria Embankment, London, EC4Y 0DZ

Orders: please contact Hachette UK Distribution, Hely Hutchinson Centre, Milton Road, Didcot, Oxfordshire, OX11 7HH. Telephone: +44 (0)1235 827827. Email education@hachette.co.uk. Lines are open from 9 a.m. to 5 p.m., Monday to Friday. You can also order through our website: www.hoddereducation.co.uk

© Gareth Holt 2019

ISBN 978-1-5104-5145-2

First printed 2019

Impression number 5 4 3

Year 2023

Questions in the Q&A section used with permission of WJEC.

Cover photo: zhu difeng/Adobe Stock

Typeset by Integra Software Services Pvt. Ltd., Pondicherry, India

Printed and bound by CPI Group (UK) Ltd, Croydon, CR0 4YY

Hachette UK's policy is to use papers that are natural, renewable and recyclable products and made from wood grown in well-managed forests and other controlled sources. The logging and manufacturing processes are expected to conform to the environmental regulations of the country of origin.

Contents

Getting the most from this book

Exam tips

Advice on key points in the text to help you learn and recall content, avoid pitfalls, and polish your exam technique in order to boost your grade.

Knowledge check

Rapid-fire questions throughout the Content Guidance section to check your understanding.

Knowledge check answers

1 Turn to the back of the book for the Knowledge check answers.

Summaries

- Each core topic is rounded off by a bullet-list summary for quick-check reference of what you need to know.

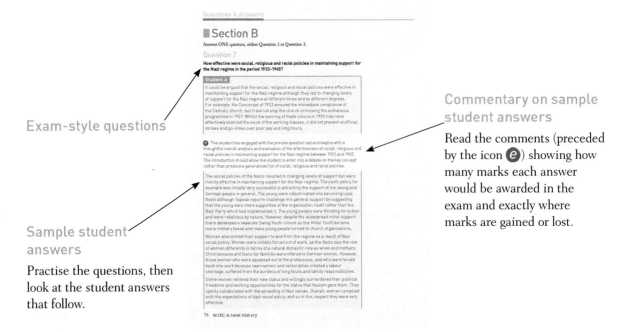

Exam-style questions

Sample student answers

Practise the questions, then look at the student answers that follow.

Commentary on sample student answers

Read the comments (preceded by the icon **e**) showing how many marks each answer would be awarded in the exam and exactly where marks are gained or lost.

■ About this book

This guide covers A-level Unit 4 Option 8 Germany: Democracy and Dictatorship c.1918–1945; Part 2: Nazi Germany c.1933–1945 in the WJEC GCE specification, which is worth 20% of the total A-level. This is the second half of the chosen depth study, the first half of which has been studied in Unit 2. Knowledge and understanding previously learnt in Unit 2 should be utilised when addressing the study of Unit 4.

The **Content Guidance** section outlines the key content areas within the period 1933–45. The first part of this section focuses on further developments in the Nazi control of Germany after 1933. It goes on to explore the impact of Nazi racial, social and religious policies between 1933 and 1945, and analyses the effectiveness of Nazi economic policy in those years. The next part of the option deals with changing Nazi foreign policy 1933–45, analysing the backdrop to the outbreak of the Second World War and evaluating the key developments during the war and the overall impact upon Germany.

The **Questions & Answers** section gives examples of responses to the extended-answer (worth 30 marks) questions in Q1 and Q2 or Q3, which focus upon the value of historical sources to a historian for a specific development and a choice of traditional essay type questions. Examples of both strong (A-grade) and weak (C-grade) responses to both types of question are provided. It is not possible to provide sample questions and answers for every development, so you must be aware that any part of the specification could be tested in the examination. This guide cannot go into full detail on every development, so you should use it alongside other resources, such as class notes and articles in journals, as well as at least some of the books included in the reading list drawn up by the WJEC for this specification.

Content Guidance

■ Chronology of Nazi Germany 1933–45

Year	Date	Event
1933	30 January	Hitler becomes Reich chancellor
	27 February	Reichstag fire
	28 February	Reichstag Fire Decree
	5 March	Reichstag election
	21 March	Day of Potsdam ceremony
	23 March	Enabling Act
	1 April	National boycott of Jewish businesses
	7 April	Law for the Restoration of the Professional Civil Service
	2 May	Trade unions abolished
	10 May	Burning of un-German books
	22 June	SPD abolished
	14 July	Law preventing the formation of parties
		Compulsory sterilisation legalised
	20 July	Concordat with Catholic church
	14 October	Germany leaves the League of Nations
	12 November	One-party election
1934	30 June	Night of the Long Knives
	2 August	Death of President Hindenburg
	19 August	Hitler becomes Führer and Reich chancellor
	24 October	German Labour Front established
1935	16 March	Conscription reintroduced
	15 September	Nuremberg Laws
1936	7 March	Remilitarisation of the Rhineland
	1 October	Four-Year Plan
1937	5 November	Hitler presents his view of foreign policy (Hossbach Memorandum)
1938	11 March	Anschluss with Austria
	29 September	Munich Conference
	1 October	Czech crisis: Sudetenland occupied
	9 November	Kristallnacht

Year	Date	Event
1939	15 March	Remainder of Czechoslovakia occupied
	23 August	Nazi–Soviet Non-Aggression Pact (Molotov–Ribbentrop Pact)
	1 September	German invasion of Poland
	3 September	Britain and France declare war on Germany
1940	22 June	French surrender/armistice with Germany
	July–October	Battle of Britain
1941	22 June	German invasion of the Soviet Union
	7 December	The USA enters the war
1942	20 January	Wannsee Conference
	13 February	Albert Speer becomes armaments minister
	23 August 1942–2 February 1943	Battle of Stalingrad
1944	6 June	D-Day invasion
	20 July	Stauffenberg's bomb plot
1945	30 April	Hitler commits suicide
	7–8 May	German armed forces surrender to the Allies

■ Key figures in Nazi Germany 1933–45

Figure	Role
Ludwig Beck	Chief of the army general staff between 1935 and 1938. He resigned over Hitler's plans to invade Czechoslovakia and became an active opponent of the Nazis.
Joseph Goebbels	Minister of propaganda and enlightenment between 1933 and 1945. He controlled the media and influenced the culture of Nazi Germany.
Hermann Göring	Minister-president of Prussia and minister for aviation 1933–45. President of the Reichstag from 1934. Responsible for the Four-Year Plan.
Reinhard Heydrich	Chief of the Reich Main Security Office, and one of the architects of the Holocaust.
Paul von Hindenburg	Elected president after Friedrich Ebert's death in 1925 and re-elected in 1932. He appointed Hitler chancellor on 30 January 1933.
Adolf Hitler	As leader of the Nazi Party he transformed a fringe party into a mass movement, eventually securing the chancellorship in January 1933.
Alfred Hugenberg	A leading nationalist and industrialist with extensive media interests, leader of the DNVP and a member of Hitler's cabinet in 1933.
Franz von Papen	A conservative politician who served as chancellor in 1932. He played a leading role in bringing Hitler to power when he persuaded Hindenburg that they could keep Hitler under their control.
Ernst Röhm	Chief of staff of the rapidly expanding SA. He was executed during the Nazi purge of June 1934.
Joachim von Ribbentrop	Foreign minister from February 1938 until 1945. He was found guilty of war crimes at Nuremberg and was hanged.
Hjalmar Schacht	President of the Reichsbank in 1933 and economics minister from 1934. He played a major role in Germany's economic recovery until his resignation in 1937.
Albert Speer	An architect and close associate of Hitler who became minister of armaments and war production in 1942.
Claus von Stauffenberg	An army officer who became disillusioned with the Nazi regime. He was a leading conspirator in the bomb plot of 1944.

■ The main political parties in the Reichstag, March 1933

KPD

The German Communist Party advocated revolution on the Russian model for Germany.

SPD

The Social Democratic Party had been the majority socialist party and the largest political party in Germany for most of the Weimar period. The SPD was an ardent supporter of a republican system of government and sought to establish a socialist state through democratic means.

DDP

The German Democratic Party was a left-wing, social liberal party, committed to democratic government and sympathetic to the Weimar Republic.

Wirtschaftspartei

The Reich Party of the German middle class, more commonly known as the Wirtschaftspartei or WP, was a conservative party set up by lower-middle-class groups.

Centre

The German Centre Party, a Catholic party (also known as Zentrum), represented the interests of the Catholic church. It was linked to the Bavarian People's Party (BVP), which represented the interests of the Catholic church in Bavaria.

BVP

The Bavarian People's Party was a Catholic party linked to the Centre Party, from which it had broken away in 1918.

DVP

The German People's Party rejected the Republic and favoured the restoration of the monarchy in Germany. It represented the interests of big business.

DNVP

The German National People's Party was a right-wing conservative party that opposed the Republic and wanted a return to an authoritarian system of government.

NSDAP

The National Socialist German Workers' Party (Nazi Party). An anti-democratic party that wanted to bring down the Weimar Republic and re-establish a nationalist, authoritarian government.

Developments in the Nazi control of Germany after 1933

Trying to ride a tiger

Coalition theory maintains that the formation of a new administration is the result of a bargaining game that is influenced by a number of interrelated critical factors. Firstly, there will be a distinct contextual environment created by both internal and external issues. Secondly, there will be specific political preferences that will shape the direction a new coalition takes. Finally, there will be an institutional framework that determines how a particular coalition is formed. All these critical factors appeared on the twisted path that led to the appointment of Hitler as chancellor of Germany in January 1933.

The impact of the Wall Street Crash and the resulting breakdown in the democratic system in Germany had created an environment in which National Socialism was able to flourish. The fact that there had been a gradual shift to the political right in the Weimar Republic effectively undermined the stability of successive Weimar coalitions. The right was intent on taking Germany back to a more authoritarian system of government. This made the accession of someone like Hitler that much easier.

President Hindenburg was the main political actor in the formation of the new government because the constitution empowered him to dismiss and appoint the chancellor. Nazi seizure of power is something of a misnomer because Hitler was invited into power as part of a compromise. It was effectively a marriage between right-wing political groups, the Nazi Party and President Hindenburg.

Blinded by political self-interest, the conservative right, orchestrated by Franz von Papen (chancellor for a brief period in 1932), was attempting to regain its position in Germany and believed that in Hitler it had found the means to do so. The aim of the conservative right was to use the Nazis initially to achieve a stable parliamentary majority and then set Germany on a political course of its own choosing.

Both Papen and Alfred Hugenberg (businessman, media proprietor and the leader of the DNVP) were convinced of the necessity of keeping Nazi ministers in a minority. Table 1 shows the composition of Hitler's first cabinet. With only three Nazis, who would be surrounded by eight influential conservatives and flanked by Vice-Chancellor Papen, they convinced themselves that Hitler could fairly easily be shackled. The idea of restraining Hitler and his party was, however, flawed from the start. To do so would require strong political characters with a will to maintain the safeguards that had been put in place. Politicians such as Papen soon showed little desire to rein Hitler in.

Knowledge check 1

Why did National Socialism flourish during the Depression?

Table 1 Hitler's first cabinet

Reich chancellor (Reichskanzler)	Adolf Hitler (NSDAP)
Vice-chancellor and Reich commissioner for Prussia	Franz von Papen (DNVP)
Reich foreign minister	Konstantin von Neurath (Conservative civil servant)
Reich minister of the interior	Dr Wilhelm Frick (NSDAP)
Reich minister of defence	General Werner von Blomberg (Nazi sympathiser)
Reich finance minister	Count Schwerin von Krosigk (Conservative civil servant)
Reich minister of economics and agriculture	Dr Alfred Hugenberg (DNVP)
Reich minister of labour	Franz Seldte (Stahlhelm leader)
Reich minister of mail and transport	Paul Freiherr von Eltz-Rübenach (Conservative civil servant)
Reich minister without portfolio, Reich air commissioner, Prussian minister of the interior	Hermann Göring (NSDAP)
Reich commissioner of employment	Dr Günther Gereke (Conservative civil servant)
Reich minister of justice	Dr Franz Gürtner (DNVP)

Papen's hubris was both criminal and fatal, stemming from the fact that he not only enjoyed the confidence of Hindenburg but also held the key position of minister-president of Prussia, which meant that he was Hermann Göring's boss, with control over the police and the Prussian administration. Furthermore, as vice-chancellor he had the right to be present when the chancellor presented his reports to the president. But as it proved, the chancellorship and control of the two interior ministries of the Reich and Prussia were all that Hitler needed to turn the so-called National Revolution into a National Socialist revolution.

As Prussian minister of the interior, Göring effectively had control over three-fifths of the internal administration of the Reich including the police. Wilhelm Frick, as Reich minister of the interior, had certain limited powers over the other two-fifths. With General von Blomberg, a Nazi sympathiser, as minister of defence, Hitler had little to fear from the army.

Sharing power was not part of Hitler's political vision. At the first opportunity he would take steps to achieve independence from his coalition partners and consolidate his position in the Reichstag. With hindsight it is now clear that Hitler would profit from, rather than be obstructed by, the composition of the new cabinet. Using the veneer of constitutional legality, he would destroy democracy.

Therefore, in the context of 1933 onwards, what was likely to happen to the democratic system in Germany given that Hitler:
- according to one British diplomat, was a cross between a salvationist and a gunman?
- along with his followers, had been prepared to break the law before 1933?
- wanted to strengthen the position of the NSDAP within the Reichstag so that he could force through measures that would change the constitution?
- had long professed his animosity towards democracy?
- collaborated with conservatives to access the administrative apparatus of the German state?
- had allies who were prepared to concede to the destruction of that state?

Stahlhelm A right-wing ex-servicemen's organisation of which Hindenburg was the honorary head.

Hitler's consolidation of power 1933–34

A legal or pseudo-legal revolution?

Democracy had not died on 30 January 1933, but it was certainly in need of life support.

Transitional governments often face a period of opportunity combined with acute vulnerability. Momentum needs to be built and sustained during the initial stages of a new government, and the first few weeks and months are often crucial for the success of the transition.

The coalition government formed on 30 January 1933 was just one in a long line of coalitions that had characterised the politics of the Weimar Republic, but this time it was dominated by the nationalist parties. It was effectively based upon the election results of November 1932, ironic given that support for the Nazis appeared to have peaked in July 1932 when they had won 230 seats in the Reichstag, compared with 196 in the later election. The allocation of seats following the November 1932 election is shown in Table 2.

Table 2 November 1932 Reichstag election results

Party	Number of seats
KPD	100
SPD	121
Centre	70
BVP	20
DDP	2
DVP	11
DNVP	52
NSDAP	196
Others	12

As for Hitler, he may have been chancellor, but his position was far from fireproof. The Nazis did not have an overall majority in the Reichstag. Hitler could potentially be dismissed at any time by the authority of the president — precisely the fate of the three previous chancellors. If he was intent on pursuing absolute power, there were a number of obstacles that he would have to overcome. He needed to:

- be able to bypass presidential authority and so increase his leverage over the president
- have unprecedented access to full legislative powers, so that he could eliminate the Reichstag as an effective organ of government
- strip away any constitutional guarantees so that he could remove the influence of the political opposition and Nazify central government
- deal with conflicting interests within the Nazi Party that threatened to destabilise his authority.

Furthermore, the Nazis were operating under certain constraints. Given that Hindenburg openly resented Hitler, any changes would have to be gradual and seem legitimate because Hitler did not want to give the president an excuse to dismiss him. Neither did he want to provoke the intervention of the army — his experience of the failed Munich Putsch of November 1923, which had led to his brief imprisonment, had taught him a lesson about risking everything on a dramatic attempt at insurrection. He would also have to tolerate the traditional political elites, despite calls from radicals in his movement to depose them. He would use the army, bureaucracy and industrialists as required in order to strengthen his power base.

Hitler did not want to approach the president with a cap in one hand and a begging bowl in the other to try to win access to the powers of a presidential decree. He realised that securing an overall parliamentary majority would be the surest way to consolidate his power. He reasoned that early elections in March 1933 could secure an overall majority and free him from dependence on Hindenburg and the other nationalist parties. It would also legitimise his regime by creating a veneer of legality and popular acceptance.

When he became chancellor, Hitler had suggested that he would try to secure the support of the Centre Party to establish a working nationalist coalition. However, he ensured that the negotiations with the Centre Party were not productive and so was able to orchestrate the dissolution of the Reichstag and the calling of immediate new elections for 5 March 1933.

In this way, both Papen and Hugenberg were outmanoeuvred. The non-Nazis in the cabinet meekly submitted, rather than challenging the calling of such a hasty election. In this they were undoubtedly guilty of conceding to Hitler, given that they could have employed a constitutional mechanism for blocking the election, via the Committee for the Protection of Parliamentary Rights.

In a free and fair election, all political actors should compete on an equitable basis, so that voters can choose freely between them. The whole electoral process should be transparent, and should ensure that all political rights are tolerated and protected, and that there is a general acceptance of the principle of free debate. It is a basic political freedom to allow and not interfere with the political messages of other parties.

However, the Nazi Party's track record, especially during the campaigns for the July and November 1932 elections, suggested it was unlikely that the five weeks of campaigning would be free and equitable.

The Nazis were keen from the outset to spread the message that social order was under threat from an imminent Communist uprising. The spectre of Communist-inspired revolution had been present throughout the Weimar period and so was an easy card for the Nazis to play. Support for the KPD had increased during the Weimar years, with the November 1932 election returning the party's best result of 100 seats. If Hitler was able to 'find' evidence of far-left insurrectionist activity during the March election campaign, he could use it to discredit the KPD and to justify taking trenchant measures against the Communist Party.

Political violence characterised the first few weeks of the election campaign. In 1932, Papen as chancellor had lifted the ban on the Sturmabteilung (SA) which was now free to administer violence with impunity as old political rivals and left-wingers were rounded up and taken into 'protective custody'. The Nazis adopted a campaign slogan of 'The restoration of order' — a clever political ploy intended to appeal to patriotic German people, while allowing brutality to masquerade as the enforcement of order.

Presidential decree
Under Article 48 of the Weimar Constitution, the president could suspend the Reichstag and rule by decree in the case of an emergency.

Committee for the Protection of Parliamentary Rights
One of the checks and balances established by the Weimar Constitution. The committee could have challenged Hitler's demand for an immediate election in March 1933, arguing that it was unreasonably hasty.

Knowledge check 2

What evidence is there that support for the KPD had grown between 1930 and 1933?

Sturmabteilung (SA)
The Nazi Party's violent paramilitary organisation. Its members were known as Brownshirts after the colour of their uniform.

As Prussian minister of the interior, Göring was able rapidly to extend Nazi control over the police and civil service in Prussia and recruited 50,000 police auxiliaries to assist the SA and the Schutzstaffel (SS) in the maintenance of law and order. He also issued an order referred to in *The Times* on 2 February 1933 as the 'shooting decree'. Another decree on 4 February made it possible to suppress and control the newspapers and public meetings of the political opposition. The meetings of the pro-republican parties and the left could not count on police protection and many left-wing politicians were beaten up.

The Nazis had almost complete control over radio broadcasting leading up to the elections. This, together with the decree of 4 February, made it very hard for the opposition to present an effective case against the NSDAP. The ability of the KPD and SPD to run effective campaigns had been severely handicapped, and it was in an increasingly anti-Communist atmosphere that the people went to the polls. Clearly the Nazis were beginning to strip the country of its constitutional liberties.

For his part and in the face of some public criticism, Hitler feigned moderation, calling upon the German people to be both cautious and patient. He claimed that the violence was the responsibility of a radical minority within the Nazi Party rather than an outbreak of state-orchestrated terror.

The Reichstag fire, 27 February 1933

As we have seen, Hitler had favoured an approach of subverting established democratic institutions from within rather than openly attempting to overthrow them, a strategy which meant that the legislature would be responsible for its own demise and a veneer of legality could be maintained. If anything, however, the events and decrees of February 1933 devalued the Nazi concept of a legal revolution. Legality, if it existed, was only ever wafer-thin — this was better defined as a pseudo-legal revolution.

Given this audit trail and in the light of what happened next, it seems implausible that the Nazis merely responded to a planned act of Communist terrorism in February 1933. But the question of responsibility has stoked the boilers of historical controversy for generations.

On 27 February 1933 the Reichstag building was engulfed by fire. The Reichstag was the physical representation of democracy in Germany. An arson attack on such a symbol amounted to an indirect attack on the people of Germany. The Nazis could not miss such an opportunity (even if events had been stage-managed) to lay the blame at the feet of their bitterest political enemies. According to the Nazi propaganda machine, the fire was started by the Communists as the initial step of a wider Communist uprising with its sights on overthrowing the government. The accusation meant that the flames of anti-Communist and anti-KPD sentiment were fanned even higher.

While the debate continues about who started the fire, there is no doubt who profited from it. The timing could not have been better, giving the Nazis scope to act against their opponents just before the election. Hitler persuaded Hindenburg to agree to a decree that would suspend most civil and political liberties. The Decree for the Protection of the People and State (also known as the Reichstag Fire Decree) was

Schutzstaffel (SS) A paramilitary group originally created to provide security for Hitler and the party, which expanded into the Nazis' main apparatus of control and state-sponsored terror.

Knowledge check 3

What was the shooting decree?

Pseudo-legal revolution Refers to the fact that Hitler would build a dictatorship based on the powers of a permanent state of emergency provided by Article 48 of the Weimar Constitution.

Knowledge check 4

Who was blamed for starting the Reichstag fire?

issued on 28 February 1933, the day following the fire. It provided the state with unprecedented powers of search, arrest, imprisonment and censorship — intended, it was claimed, as purely temporary measures.

In an apparent show of legality and seeming adherence to the constitution, the Communists were allowed to contest the 5 March election, even though the KPD had been named as being responsible for the fire. However, this was not adherence to a democratic principle, but merely a tactical gesture, further reinforcing the impression that the Nazis were prepared to listen to the will of the people.

There was nothing fair or equitable about the 5 March election given the inability of the SPD and KPD to campaign freely. The election results (shown in Table 3) unsurprisingly confirmed that the Nazis had increased their share of the popular vote from 33.1% in November 1932 to 43.9% in 1933. They had won 288 seats, but had still failed to gain an overall majority.

Table 3 March 1933 Reichstag election results

Party	Number of seats
KPD	81
SPD	120
Centre	74
BVP	18
DDP	5
DVP	2
DNVP	52
NSDAP	288
Others	7

However, by 9 March Nazi officials had seized power in the Länder and the last traces of autonomy for the German states were quashed, with the destruction of local state government by Frick and the creation of Reich governors.

The Nazi state was centralised by the abolition of the Reichsrat (the upper house of the Reichstag) on 30 January 1934. This was a plain breach of the Weimar Constitution and revealed that Nazi rule had been imposed on a local level throughout Germany before the dictatorship had been established in the centre. Germany had now become a national rather than a federal state.

However, the election result meant that Hitler was still reliant upon the compliance of the president and the Reichstag. As Article 68 of the Weimar Constitution stated, 'Reich laws shall be enacted by the Reichstag'. If Hitler was to assume more dictatorial power, he would have to find a way to bypass the legislative powers of the Reichstag and usurp the political authority of Hindenburg.

The Enabling Act, 23 March 1933

From democracy to dictatorship

It is claimed that Hitler had developed plans for an Enabling Act following the disappointing outcome of the November 1932 elections. If this was the case, then the

Knowledge check 5

Why did the Nazis allow the KPD to contest the 5 March election if the Communists were guilty of setting the Reichstag fire?

Exam tip

Ultimately the Nazis had no intention of adhering to the outcome of the election in any shape or form, so allowing opposition parties to take part made no great difference, apart from maintaining the illusion of a 'legal revolution'.

Länder Germany's largely self-governing states.

National rather than federal Germany had a strong tradition of devolution of authority from the centre to the states. The federal system was made up of independent, largely self-governing states within a unitary Reich. This process was reversed to create a fully united, centralised Nazi state.

Exam tip

It is a good approach to point out that in the course of 1933–34 Hitler systematically pursued a policy of Gleichschaltung, which meant bringing German society into line.

preparatory work for the act was already well underway with the help of civil servants — meaning that bureaucrats had colluded with Hitler and paved the way for his assumption of dictatorial powers.

The Enabling Act, or 'The Law for Removing the Distress of the People and Reich', was passed by 441 votes to 94 on 23 March 1933. The act gave the chancellor powers to enact laws without the involvement of the Reichstag — or the decree-making powers of the president. The provisions were meant to be for a period of four years, but were in reality the prelude to the establishment of a Nazi dictatorship in a one-party state.

The act was considered an amendment to the constitution. Under Weimar constitutional law, any amendments to the constitution had to be approved by a two-thirds majority in the Reichstag. However, the 5 March election results were such that the Nazis did not have the necessary two-thirds majority even with the support of the DNVP. This would have to be secured by other means.

The steps taken to ensure the act received sufficient support in the Reichstag (now meeting in the Kroll Opera House) included the following:

- The Communist deputies, who could have been expected to vote against the bill, had been excluded from the Reichstag by the Reichstag Fire Decree and were therefore unable to vote.
- Some SPD deputies had been arrested, and others may have been intimidated by the presence of the SA during the vote. The SPD was the only party that voted against the Enabling Act.
- The Nazis depended on the support of the Centre Party. At Potsdam two days earlier, on 21 March, the SA and SS had stood in solemn discipline and an impressive show of legality. This image of traditionalism, together with assurances about the future status of the Roman Catholic faith in Germany, reassured the Centre Party into voting for the Enabling Act.

Thus a democratic party drove the final nail into the Weimar constitutional coffin because it lacked the willpower and determination to keep liberty alive.

Again, Hitler had acted with the appearance of legality, but the Enabling Act's constitutional validity has been challenged. Most significantly, it was passed by a Reichstag that was not fully constituted. The exclusion of the Communist deputies breached legislative procedure and should therefore have invalidated the suspension of the constitution.

Hitler had lulled all those whose cooperation he had needed with understandings that now evaporated. Firmly in control of the police, the SS and the SA, he could now, under the shadow of official sanction, eliminate the remaining obstacles to total power. He had destroyed the Reichstag as an effective democratic institution and the next step was to destroy the other political parties.

On 26 May the Communist Party was abolished and its deputies arrested. Since Hitler had eliminated the Communists, it was feasible that the traditional right might now choose to get rid of Hitler and establish a presidential dictatorship. After voting to ban the KPD the DNVP was also forced to dissolve itself on 27 June.

Exam tip

The naming of Nazi legislation was more concerned with marketing National Socialism than with clarity about what each law did.

Potsdam The opening ceremony for the new government was held at Potsdam in a symbolic ceremony that demonstrated the unity of the old order with the new, personified in Hindenburg and Hitler. The semblance of order lulled the German people and politicians into a false sense of security.

The nationalists were squeezed out of government and the Centre Party and the SPD were dissolved. The so-called conservative framework that had been built to contain Hitler was now destroyed. The whole process culminated in the law of 14 July 1933, which made it a political offence to organise any political grouping outside the NSDAP.

In November 1933 another election was held, and unsurprisingly the Nazis took all the seats in the Reichstag because the electorate was offered a single party list for its approval. Thus Germany officially became a one-party state and a law established the unity of party and state in December 1933.

The Night of the Long Knives, 30 June 1934

By 1934, the idea that rule of law would underpin the power of the Nazi government was replaced by the principles of National Socialist philosophy. In effect it meant that Nazis could justify any action under the veil of a permanent state of emergency. The normal function of orderly, reasoned government was to be by-passed by the arbitrary exercise of power through Hitler.

Following the political developments of 1933, the only obstacles remaining between Hitler and total power were the German army, Hindenburg and the radical wing of the Nazi Party.

Superficially it might seem that the army and the SA were both synonymous with National Socialism. However, their relationship was not straightforward. The leadership of the army was drawn from within the old aristocratic right-wing. Many army leaders were still dubious about the threat the Nazis posed to social and political order, and Hitler would have to work to win their support.

As for the SA, the independent attitude of Röhm, its leader, threatened Hitler's position. Röhm not only hoped to create what was in effect an SA state via a 'second revolution', but wanted to subsume the German army within the ranks of the SA under his own leadership.

> **Knowledge check 6**
>
> What was Röhm's 'second revolution'?

Hindenburg, for his part, had never shown any love for Hitler and National Socialism. Although he played a diminished role as president since the passing of the Enabling Act, he still wielded enormous influence within Germany.

In June 1934 all three potential obstacles intersected. The imminent death of Hindenburg made it imperative that Hitler acted to secure the support of the army before attempting to assimilate the president's powers. Hitler did not want another conservative president foisted on him by the traditional right. Neither did he want the army to combine with other conservative elements to veto his possible succession to Hindenburg. He needed a strategy that could protect his political gains, win the support of the army, and nullify the radical wing of the SA led by Röhm.

The result was a purge known as the Night of the Long Knives. Between 30 June and 2 July 1934, Röhm and other leading stormtroopers were murdered as well as a number of conservatives including former chancellor Kurt von Schleicher and his wife. Other victims included Gregor Strasser, a left-wing Nazi, and the Centre Party leader Erich Klausener.

The purge removed the potential for the SA to become an alternative power base and set a precedent for state-sponsored extra-judicial killings. Murder exploded across Germany as the Nazis took the opportunity to settle old scores, revealing their propensity for injustice, arbitrary rule and government by crime. Nevertheless, there was an attempt to give the purge retrospective legality through a decree, approved by the cabinet on 3 July, stating that the measures which had been taken were legal as acts of self-defence by the state against treasonable plots. In conservative circles, the purge was welcomed as a necessary intervention to restore order.

The army, which regarded the SA as a dangerous rival, had backed the purge (whose victims included at least one general), providing weapons and logistical support. The army was thus deeply compromised by the events, and had played an important part in Hitler's consolidation of power. However, the decisive actions of the Night of the Long Knives had been taken by the new force emerging in Germany, the SS. Although still nominally part of the SA, the SS had begun to take the opportunity to stir up mutual suspicions between the SA and the army in the build-up to the events of 30 June.

> **Exam tip**
>
> The purge of 30 June 1934 should be seen as a pragmatic move to avoid the possibility of a military coup involving conservative forces and the German army.

The impact of the death of Hindenburg

Five weeks later, on 2 August 1934, Hindenburg died, and Hitler combined the offices of president and chancellor into one as Führer and Reichskanzler (Reich chancellor). He defied his own Enabling Act by combining the two offices of state and took the opportunity to revise his relationship with the army, exacting an oath of unconditional loyalty from them. Exceeding his authority, General Blomberg ensured that the oath was made to Hitler as an individual. This was yet another constitutional violation, because the pledge of loyalty should have been made to the state and the constitution.

On 19 August 1934, a plebiscite approved the union of the offices of state. The final farce of the pseudo-legal revolution was enacted when 38 million Germans gave their public assent to Hitler's assumption of power as Führer and Reichskanzler. Even at this stage, the Nazis felt it necessary to provide a veneer of legality to underwrite their seizure of power.

> **Plebiscite** A referendum — a vote by the people to secure popular approval of a policy or development.

Propaganda, indoctrination and terror

Propaganda and its limits

A dictatorship will strive to create a kind of uniformity of thought, discouraging any form of individualism or diversity of viewpoint. A prime target for any dictatorship will therefore be to control the channels of mass media and all institutions that project attitudes, values or beliefs.

Techniques of propaganda and indoctrination work best when combining the most up-to-date technology with psychological pressure, and are most effective when directed towards people who are already insecure and vulnerable. In 1930s Germany there was a ready-made audience in a society that was still suffering from a deep sense of national humiliation and which was damaged by inflation, economic depression and mass unemployment.

The public mood can be both fickle and febrile, so that the propaganda message will need frequent adjustment to fit the current agenda. Indeed, if a regime is to convince people that it is not trying to deceive them, it will have to turn exaggeration and untruths into an art form. The political language of Nazism was short, sharp and intense, designed to appeal to pack instincts, and stripped of any necessity for explanation or debate.

In Nazi Germany the man responsible for propaganda was Joseph Goebbels, who headed the Ministry of Popular Culture and Enlightenment. In his attempt to engineer uniformity of thought and action he worked towards establishing 'total propaganda'. Essentially, he divided the nation into actives and passives, members and sympathisers. His aim was to enlarge the group of sympathisers and retain the members, because propaganda was as much about confirming and consolidating the views and prejudices of those who already sympathised as about converting those who didn't.

The press and radio were the two main pillars of communication, but the Nazis were keen to use any institution and all techniques of persuasion to conquer the German masses, including schools, universities and the Hitler Youth. Film was used as a direct propaganda weapon. Leni Riefenstahl, for example, produced a glorified image of Hitler in *The Triumph of the Will* (1935).

The central goal of Nazi propaganda was to radically reconstruct German society and manufacture a new Volksgemeinschaft or 'national community', inspired by a vision of an idealised past of which the hallmarks were a heightened sense of unity and a pure racial community. The Nazi propaganda machine constantly urged the population to put the community before the individual, and the notion of a national community went hand in hand with the Führer myth.

It has been suggested that, through a well-functioning propaganda and indoctrination machine, the Nazis were able to brainwash all those German people who would otherwise have resisted Nazism. However, to accept this is also to imply that the German people were capable of being entirely seduced by propaganda. It is difficult to believe that propaganda alone could have sustained the party and its ideology over a period of 12 years. Moreover, it is quite possible that the impact of propaganda and indoctrination has been exaggerated. If the press and radio were the two pillars of Nazi propaganda, journalism became bland and one-dimensional, causing a decline in public interest. Between 1933 and 1939 there was a 10% decline in newspaper circulation. In 1932 only 25% of German households owned a wireless. You cannot be directly influenced by media that you do not have access to.

In reality, it is likely that some Germans supported the Nazis primarily because doing so served their own interests, and that Nazi propaganda was as effective as it was because it reflected many of the aspirations of a section of the German populace.

In other words, propaganda was preaching, at least in some cases, to the partially converted, who could identify with the Nazi vision of resurgent militarism, nationalism and social conservatism. Propaganda rhetoric in its many forms and incantations provided a sugar-coated image of the perfect society where hope and opportunity were accessible to all true Germans.

Volksgemeinschaft A radical transformation of German society into a national community (or people's community) based on racial conformity and hierarchy.

Führer myth Hitler was seen as the embodiment of the will of the German people, a man with a combination of iron determination and messianic leadership qualities.

Exam tip

Challenge the view that popular support for the Nazi regime was mainly the result of effective propaganda.

Censorship

It is unlikely that the Nazis believed propaganda and indoctrination alone would change social, economic, political and cultural conditions within Germany. They would have to be used in conjunction with other tools such as censorship and terror.

As any form of social, political, economic or cultural dissent or non-conformity had the potential to expose the abuses of the ruling government, the Nazis were bound to make extensive use of censorship. Cultural life was muzzled. Books written by those of different persuasions or designated 'non-persons' were banned and burned, and the works of 2,500 important writers, such as Thomas Mann, were denounced and forbidden. The works of 'degenerate artists' were at first displayed and publicly derided and then confiscated. Völkisch music and the grand operas of Wagner were promoted to establish an emotional bond between the party and the people.

Völkisch From German folk tradition.

Repression, fear and violence

Intimidation and surveillance are at the core of any dictatorship and the Third Reich was no exception. Those whom propaganda could not reach, the Nazis sought to control through the increasing use of terror and coercion. The Gestapo, Sicherheitsdienst (SD), concentration camps, the People's Court and 'protective custody' were used to brutalise the nation and nullify dissent. Preventive policing enabled the Nazis to root out and eliminate potential opposition. Ordinary people were encouraged to denounce their neighbours. Terror effectively became institutionalised and the destruction of independent organisations made it easier for the regime to reduce the potential for people to stand together against Nazi tyranny.

Sicherheitsdienst (SD) The intelligence service of the SS and the Nazi Party.

People's Court A court established in April 1934 to deal with cases of treason.

For some German people, however, the use of terror was an acceptable means of dealing with 'deviant' behaviour. The Nazi propaganda machine naturally encouraged this line of thought, marginalising its victims and portraying them as criminals, traitors and asocials. Concentration camps were presented as a necessary evil, or even beneficial because they turned asocials into good Germans through work and discipline. Communists, of course, were simply getting what they deserved.

Asocials Social groups or individuals who were seen as a genetic or moral threat to the national community.

Many German people were no doubt intimidated by the use of terror because it reinforced their defencelessness in the absence of genuine law, order and justice. The pervasive fear of violence should not be underestimated. When you add to this a tradition of obedience within German society it is easier to understand why many German people gave popular consent to a regime that fundamentally went against their best interests.

The Nazi political system

If we accept the premise that each country has its own political context and culture, it could be argued that the Weimar Republic was an aberration in German political history, in that it was a period of democracy which followed an unbroken pattern of authoritarian government. Given widespread disillusionment with democracy, and the fact that in its wilderness years the Nazi Party had presented itself as a revolutionary movement that was both anti-liberal and anti-democratic, it would not have come as a great surprise to the German people that the Nazis reintroduced an older political platform with new institutional faces.

In the transition from the Weimar Republic to the Third Reich, the authority of the Reichstag and any free political expression were early casualties. The abolition of the Reichsrat removed the historic subdivisions of imperial Germany. Germany had become a national instead of a federal state.

The Reich cabinet did not meet after February 1938 and had become a mere sounding board for Hitler. The Führerprinzip established Hitler's absolute authority. It provided him in principle with exclusive and unlimited power. The army's oath of allegiance was to Hitler and not the state. Hitler had claimed that authoritarian rule through the Nazi Party would create better, more organised government. The Hitler myth depicted him as the omnipresent, omnicompetent leader whose authority was undisputed and undiluted. Nazi propaganda furnished him with supernatural qualities of leadership.

However, appearances can be deceptive. Behind the façade of an ordered dictatorship with Hitler in complete control was a country that effectively had two government administrations. Both central and local government witnessed a surprising degree of continuity as the former ministries were retained and the traditional civil service continued to function.

There was no attempt to destroy all the existing institutions and replace them with Nazi organs because Hitler was not over-enthusiastic about making Nazi Party control so powerful that it could threaten his own authority. Neither was he, on the other hand, keen to allow the traditional civil service to monopolise the administrative bureaucracy. But he needed to make use of its traditions of competence and expertise to administer and implement constitutional and legal procedures within government. The Law for the Restoration of the Professional Civil Service of April 1933 removed Jewish people and known opponents from the civil service, yet Nazism lacked either the capacity or the willingness to bring in a complete institutional reorganisation of the bureaucracy.

Fundamentally, Hitler's solution was to integrate parallel institutions from within the Nazi Party and the old civil service. Existing institutions were not destroyed but shadowed by Nazi organs of state, which led to overlapping and duplication. (The same pattern emerged in central and local government.) The established civil service wanted to protect its longstanding traditions while ensuring that the bureaucratic machine functioned smoothly. It did not welcome the interference of unqualified party elements. Nazi Party functionaries, for their part, were keen to enforce the Führer's edicts and often assumed the responsibility of working towards what they assumed Hitler wanted.

The result was that an institutional civil war developed. German government became a cockpit of rival forces squabbling over the extent of their responsibilities. For example, the general inspector for roads came into conflict with the minister of transport; the youth leader of the Reich competed with the minister of education.

The extent of totalitarian control

While historians have used totalitarianism as a useful label to describe the Nazi regime, they have found it harder to define exactly what is meant by a totalitarian regime. The debate revolves around whether such a regime is defined by its bureaucracy, ideology, terror or the psychopathology of the leader. Perhaps a simpler

Führerprinzip An idea that actually pre-dated the Nazis, this was the principle of absolute obedience to the leader and complete acceptance of whatever decisions he reached. It placed Hitler's word above the written law.

Exam tip

Understand that the traditional civil service must share responsibility for the many crimes committed by the Third Reich. The bureaucracy at the heart of the administration collaborated with the SS, big business and the army.

synthesis would conclude that it is a government that maintains a totality of power given the resources of the twentieth century, or the complete envelopment of a society by the political system.

Carl J. Friedrich's Six Point Syndrome could be described as a blend of all of the above. In *The Unique Character of Totalitarian Society* Friedrich expounded six key features of a totalitarian government: a single mass party led by one man, a complete monopoly of control by the party, an official ideology, a monopoly over mass communications, a system of terrorist police control, and central control and direction over the economy.

This is a logical starting point for any discussion about totalitarianism because it means that non-totalitarian regimes can have totalitarian features. However, it has been argued that this approach is flawed because it is too static and final. It does not consider changes or developments in the inner dynamics of a system of government.

If we use Friedrich's yardstick, it would seem that the Third Reich possessed at least the main features of a totalitarian state, but how effectively they operated is the subject of ongoing debate.

A single mass party led by one man?

Hitler most certainly held totalitarian ambitions but the extent to which he achieved them is open to question. Although it would seem, at least superficially, that there was a single mass party led by one man in Nazi Germany, the idea that Hitler was the undisputed leader has been criticised as far too one-dimensional. Indeed, the image of Hitler as an omnipotent and omnipresent leader is misleading, and the view that he established an ordered monolithic state has been challenged.

The power of a dictator will always be tested by the practical difficulties of trying to keep up with, let alone controlling, everything that is going on. This was particularly so for Hitler because he was essentially lazy and hated the practical business of government. He would therefore have to rely upon mini-Hitlers, acolytes and sycophants, to deal with the everyday business of government. Furthermore, the fact that he allowed two administrative structures to function alongside each other, namely the state and the traditional civil service, meant that two parallel hierarchies were effectively doing the same job. This would inevitably lead to overlaps and inefficiency.

If we accept the premise that Hitler organised things this way to make himself supreme arbiter in a divide and rule administration, this would suggest that he retained overall authority and was a strong leader.

However, if we challenge that premise, and argue that the situation was simply a by-product of his ineffective leadership, this could be offered as evidence of neglect and weakness in the running of the country, which led in effect to authoritarian anarchy. This contrasts strongly with the idea that totalitarian rule would create better, more efficient government.

Divide and rule Hitler deliberately weakened his rivals by turning them against each other. He maintained authority because of the confusion and conflict he created.

A complete monopoly of control by the party?

There may have been only one tolerated party, which was an instrument of totalitarian control, but it was never allowed to assume total control. In his vision of totalitarianism, Hitler devised a system of controlled autonomy, which meant that while he would use the Nazi Party as a pillar for support, he would never allow it to become strong enough to rival his own position.

A monopoly over mass communications?

Hitler certainly created a monopoly of control over mass communications, but was never able to establish complete uniformity of thought because there would always be pockets of resistance. As the Second World War dragged on, the government had increasingly to resort to threats and coercion, which demonstrates the limits of Nazi propaganda and the collapse of any sort of national consensus.

Central control and direction over the economy?

The Nazis were not able to establish complete control and direction over the economy throughout the duration of the regime, because there developed a mixture of state and private capitalism.

An official ideology?

There was an ideology that presented Hitler's vision to the German people, but the ideas were all part of the manipulation of the people and not the complete essence of the regime. It could be argued that Hitler's ideology was just a variant of a set of attitudes and prejudices inherited from nationalist writers of the previous generation.

A system of terrorist police control?

The most distinctive feature of totalitarianism in Germany was the creation of a system of repressive police control in the shape of the SS. This was one of the main innovations of the Nazi system of government, allowing the systematic use of terror by the state.

In the final analysis, it has been argued that Hitler used a combination of propaganda to delude Germany's population and terror to force people into submission. However, we should challenge the assumption that Hitler exercised absolute control within a totalitarian state and that Nazism successfully penetrated every aspect of German life.

The extent of support, opposition and resistance to Nazi control

Enthusiastic support, willing acquiescence or outright hostility?

Any regime that endeavours to establish a totality of power will try to ensure that it can maintain the support of the people while eradicating the potential for opposition. Those whom it cannot deceive through propaganda, it will try to intimidate into submission through terror. A dictatorship gradually corrupts the moral fibre of its citizens, and in the Germany of the 1930s, resistance grew increasingly difficult as Nazi power became more firmly entrenched.

Silence should not be construed as acceptance, however. Internal police reports revealed that dissatisfaction with the regime was never completely eradicated. In many towns, socialist and Communist groups continued to meet. Some working-class dissatisfaction with the Third Reich persisted throughout the 1930s, even after the trade unions and left-wing political parties had been wound up. Hundreds of thousands of left-wing newspapers, pamphlets and leaflets were smuggled into Germany.

However, in the final analysis, there was a general lack of will to oppose the regime.

Support or acquiescence?

There were certainly fluctuations in the degree of consent to Nazi governance in this period, because the attitudes and experiences of German people differed widely and depended on their position in society. It is also very likely that many people were unaware of the extent to which they were being indoctrinated by the propaganda being fed to them.

Some German people willingly gave their support to Nazi ideals and policies. In terms of the overall vision, Nazi ideas were vague and flexible enough to accommodate a wide popular base of support. In some senses, National Socialism could mean different things to different people. Hitler's philosophy may have been made up of half-baked ideas and prejudices, but these were delivered with tremendous skill in oratory, and were supported, as we have seen, by effective propaganda.

The Volksgemeinschaft, or national community, had a broad appeal and would continue to foster at least passive support for the regime. It appealed to the pack instinct, providing a convenient and satisfying checklist for who was 'in', and more importantly, who was 'out'. The extreme nationalism and patriotism of Nazi propaganda created an emotional response and acted as a kind of ideological glue, binding together disparate groups who could associate their particular hopes and aspirations with the national cause. The revival of Germany implied the recovery of their own moral and material well-being.

In terms of Nazi policies, some resonated powerfully with the existing views or prejudices of sections of the population which shared the Nazis' embrace of militarism, nationalism and cultural conservatism, and their hostility towards Sinti and Roma people, homosexual people, homeless people and those labelled as 'work-shy'. Some German people may have welcomed repressive measures against groups portrayed in propaganda as deviant or intent on Communist overthrow of the state – as when the assassinations of the Night of the Long Knives were accepted by many as a reasonable measure to defend the state.

Aspects of the Nazis' economic programme were very popular. The Nazis came to power on a promise of providing bread and work for the masses. In the period 1933–36 their key aim was to reduce unemployment by investment in work-creation schemes such as land reclamation and reforestation. By mid-1935, unemployment had been reduced from over 6 million to 2.1 million.

There were also policies that had positive benefits for working-class German people. The introduction of payment by results was beneficial to healthy young workers, and the Strength Through Joy movement provided some groups of workers with decent leisure facilities and holidays. There were measures encouraging people to help their poorest fellow-citizens, such as the Winter Help campaign, which reflected the ideals of Volksgemeinschaft.

Exam tip

Both Gestapo and SOPADE reports should be treated with caution when trying to establish the degree of popular support for the Nazi regime. (SOPADE was the Social Democratic Party in exile.)

Strength Through Joy Kraft durch Freude (KdF), or Strength Through Joy, was the recreational branch of the German Labour Front.

Knowledge check 7

What was the Winter Help campaign?

In spite of such inducements, it is likely that Nazi policies had less appeal for at least some older working-class people, many of whom had been members of the SPD or KPD and of trade unions, all of which were now banned. The support of these workers would have been harder to secure.

The middle classes on the whole saw the regime as advantageous to business. Retailers could anticipate higher profits because economic improvements meant people had more money to spend. Some middle-class men benefited from job opportunities in an expanded civil service while others were able to take jobs vacated by women, or in professions from which Jewish people were excluded.

The Nazis were popular with many young people because they tapped into two contrasting aspects of the psyche of younger people. On the one hand they were able to appeal to a spirit of rebellion, because of their rejection of the intellectual world, but they also fostered and made use of youthful patriotism and a sense of duty to the Fatherland. Some women were content with the honour and prestige bestowed on them as mothers. For young men the regime at least offered employment and the potential for social mobility.

The Führer myth was fed by foreign policy successes as it became apparent that Hitler was in the process of recovering everything that had been lost at Versailles in 1919. His popularity grew along with developments such as rearmament, the plebiscite that returned the Saar area to Germany in January 1935, remilitarisation of the Rhineland in 1936, and the Anschluss with Austria and occupation of the Sudetenland, both in 1938. His status and credibility were further boosted by the willingness of European statesmen to condone these acquisitions and to negotiate with the regime.

Opposition

Although Nazi propaganda portrayed the people of Germany as marching forward in step together, in tune with Hitler's vision of 'Ein Volk, Ein Reich, Ein Führer', the reality was somewhat different. Tens of thousands of German people actively opposed or resisted the regime, but with the threat of death or imprisonment hanging over those who spoke out, resistance was not an easy option.

Ein Volk, Ein Reich, Ein Führer One people, one empire, one leader: a Nazi propaganda slogan.

Collective cowardice or a society of resisters?

Many German people who might have spoken out kept silent for the sake of their families and friends, and in so doing paradoxically helped to create an illusion of unity that strengthened the Nazi state. As a result, to some external observers, the German people were guilty of an act of collective cowardice. Others, however, argue that all German people were resisters because they were living under siege from an alien and reactionary system in the shape of National Socialism.

The truth probably falls somewhere in between, because while Allied contact with the underground movements in Germany indicated that there was extensive opposition from both sides of the political spectrum, the lack of a coordinated, coherent opposition could be interpreted as an indicator of popular support for the Nazi regime. Opposition to the Nazis tended to be fragmented, with different groups objecting to different aspects of the regime. And there were sectors of society that supported some Nazi policies while disliking others.

However, it must be remembered that the dissolution of independent organisations, such as political parties and trade unions, removed the potential for the German people to stand together against the Nazis — a hugely important factor in trying to understand the apparent acquiescence of Germans in the period 1933–45. In many ways the Nazi regime was able to engineer the passive consent of the population by actively depoliticising it, and removing the organisations that could have coordinated and voiced opposition.

As it was, those who were unwilling to submit to Nazi authority were either dismissed from their jobs or liquidated. The civil service was purged of dissident elements and independent pressure groups were taken over by the Nazis. Censorship blocked the publication and circulation of anti-Nazi views. The creation of the Labour Service also made dissent more difficult, and when war came it reinforced the hold of the Nazi regime.

Yet another factor, arguably, was the lack of a strong revolutionary tradition in Germany, in place of which was a heritage of obedience to authority.

It could still be argued that the lack of coherent opposition reveals considerable consent to the regime, and the fact that ordinary people regularly denounced their neighbours suggests that some German people were prepared to suspend their moral judgement in order to support the regime. Without such active collaboration it would have been practically impossible for the Gestapo to enforce control over the population.

However, some denouncers may have taken advantage of the opportunity to inform for selfish reasons such as settling disputes or old grudges, rather than out of devotion to the regime. Furthermore, most of the population had no direct contact with either the Gestapo or the concentration camps, which meant that many people did not witness the treatment meted out to victims of the Reich.

Clerical opposition

The church was a clear example of an institution that could approve of some Nazi policies while objecting to others. For example, many in the church could welcome attacks on Bolshevism while disapproving of the state's interference in their affairs. What they failed to grasp was that the Nazi hostility to Bolshevism was part of the same crude ideology which undermined the role and position of the church.

Opposition from within the church was left to individuals, rather than coming from the institution as a whole. This was in spite of the fact that the Christian churches had been allowed to retain organisational autonomy and that ministers and priests had the authority and the opportunity to influence their flocks in churches throughout the land. Thus, one of the organisations with the greatest potential to foment and voice resistance to the Nazis failed to do so.

The Catholic church

The Catholic church had the potential to stand independent of the regime. It was internationally based and had a network of schools, clubs and societies and youth groups. Unlike the political groups, the church could not be abolished or incorporated into the regime.

It posed a problem for the Nazi regime for various reasons. Its teachings were at odds with Nazi policies and methods. Catholics owed allegiance to the Pope (while Protestants cherished a tradition of religious independence), which implied a challenge to Hitler's authority. Bishop Galen spoke out against euthanasia and there was religious opposition to sterilisation. The clamour became so loud that Hitler had to publicly order the end of acts of euthanasia, although secretly they continued.

The Catholic church also spoke out against aspects of racial policy that might affect German families, such as eugenics, but it did not challenge fundamental Nazi ideology, as concerted Catholic opposition extended neither to anti-Semitic policies nor Lebensraum.

The Protestant church

Much of the clerical opposition to the regime was based on a single issue, as was the case in the Protestant church, which sought to defend Lutheran principles. The Protestant church was more concerned about the way religion was organised rather than the morality of the Nazi regime itself. The overall impression is that as long as they could retain their independence, a large number of Protestants were content to go along with the regime.

In summary, while both churches caused some embarrassment to the regime, neither offered the kind of vigorous opposition that might have given it genuine difficulties.

Political opposition: activism and resistance

With the creation of a one-party state, the regime successfully crushed political opposition. However, despite the speed and ruthlessness of the persecution of socialists and Communists, it was unlikely that such large numbers of left-wing sympathisers would disappear altogether. But many of the leaders who could have moulded dissent had fled abroad, particularly to Prague, Paris and London.

Patently aware of the dangers of open opposition, the socialists who remained resorted to an anti-Nazi leafleting campaign. Following another Gestapo clampdown between 1935 and 1936, the socialists were reduced to running local discussion groups that drew little attention from the authorities.

Communist resistance was equally ineffective. Their leaders had been brutally persecuted following the Reichstag Fire Decree. By 1945, over half of German Communists had been imprisoned or arrested and between 25,000 and 30,000 had been executed. The Communists therefore spent most of their time rebuilding their shattered cells rather than trying to foment unrest and disorder. The underground movement did produce anti-Nazi literature, and there was some industrial sabotage carried out by the Red Orchestra. But the signing of the Nazi–Soviet Pact in 1939 further undermined the Communist potential to offer a challenge to the regime, and there was always a ready supply of citizens willing to denounce their activities. Overall, the fact that socialists and Communists lacked a common strategy restricted the potential of the left to pose a radical threat to the Nazis.

The Nazi system entrenched support for itself through the creation of Nazified occupational organisations such as the German Labour Front and the National Socialist Teachers League, and branched into education through the National Socialist Students' League and the Hitler Youth.

Euthanasia Generally this means mercy killing, but in Nazi Germany it was a euphemism for mass murder.

Eugenics The belief that a race of people can be improved through selective breeding.

Lebensraum Literally means 'living space' but refers to territorial expansion.

Red Orchestra A subgroup of Communists engaged in resistance activities intended to subvert the Nazi war machine.

German Labour Front Following the abolition of trade unions all German workers were enrolled within the Deutsche Arbeitsfront (DAF), or German Labour Front. Its aim was to control the labour force and end disputes between management and workers.

Students and young people: dissent and nonconformity

After the Nazis came to power, membership of the Hitler Youth organisations rapidly expanded, surging to over 2 million by the end of 1933. The following year the Hitler Youth was declared the only permitted youth group in Germany, and by the end of 1936 there were more than 5 million members. With separate organisations for boys and girls, the Hitler Youth set about training them to fulfil their allotted future roles, with quasi-military training for the boys and instruction in how to be good wives and mothers for the girls.

While many young people embraced the tenets of the Hitler Youth, which promoted patriotism, nationalism and obedience to authority, others rebelled and refused to join. Some set up or joined groups that opposed the ideology of the Hitler Youth and the state.

These groups included the Edelweiss Pirates, an association of youth groups in western Germany that objected to the Nazis' endeavours to control every aspect of young people's lives. In contrast to the Hitler Youth, the Edelweiss Pirates encouraged free speech and had mixed male and female membership. During the 1930s, their activities were typically hiking and camping trips in which, away from the eyes and ears of informants, they could sing banned songs and have free discussions. After the outbreak of war, however, the authorities began to suspect them of spreading anti-Nazi messages through leaflets and graffiti, and Himmler made it clear that he wanted members of disloyal youth groups to be sent to concentration camps — along with their parents, if their parents had encouraged them — and denied any further education. In late 1944, thirteen people were publicly hanged in Cologne, six of them teenage members of the Edelweiss Pirates.

Another key youth group was the White Rose at Munich University. Its members distributed anti-Nazi leaflets and posters and organised marches. For these activities, two of its members, Hans and Sophie Scholl (who, with their other siblings, had once been keen members of the Hitler Youth) were executed in 1943 by guillotine.

While some have argued that youthful non-conformity had the potential to undermine the regime bit by bit, others have concluded that activities such as listening to jazz (particularly popular with the mainly well-off Swing Youth and Swing Jazz groups) were hardly likely to bring down the Nazis. However, the crackdown on opposition youth groups during the war, and particularly the executions in 1943 and 1944, demonstrate both the brutality of the regime and its extreme sensitivity to challenges.

Right-wing opposition: the challenges from within

Some elements of the right acted through moral conviction and a revulsion at Nazi activities, which were viewed as both anti-German and inhuman.

The armed forces could have become an engine of resistance to the regime if they had so chosen. Their opposition was of course high-risk and high-profile, and the outcome was uncertain. However, their resistance needs to be qualified: they turned against Hitler mainly because his brand of nationalism was too extreme even for them. A moderate Hitler they might find acceptable, but they could not support a Hitler who had veered out of control.

The Beck plot of 1938 and the bomb plot of 1944 (also known as the 20 July plot) were manifestations of the disillusionment of the armed forces. It should be remembered that Stauffenberg's bomb plot came to fruition pretty late in the day.

Some unhappy army officers joined the Kreisau Circle, whose members also included professionals, churchmen, politicians and scholars. Those involved in the Kreisau Circle held differing political views (many were Christian socialists) and as they were opposed to the use of force to overthrow the regime, they did not pose a serious threat.

In the final analysis, most of the groups outside the army posed very little serious threat to the functioning of the Nazi regime. And those who did oppose Hitler — for example in the army — were not necessarily searching for a democratic solution to Germany's problems.

It is of course regrettable that the majority of Germans chose to support Hitler's regime to the very end, because while many German people remained at odds with the Third Reich, only a few exceptional people, driven by a mixture of bravery, despair, disillusionment and frustration, dared to express their criticisms and opposition openly. There was no collective action against the Nazi regime. What opposition there was seems to have been most significant in private life, with groups of like-minded people meeting secretly in order to keep alive their hopes for a better future.

Beck Plot Ludwig Beck, chief of staff of the Germany army 1935–38, became disillusioned with the Nazis. He tried to persuade Britain to support his plan to arrest Hitler in 1938. But Neville Chamberlain was very dubious about getting involved, and Hitler's success at the Munich Conference basically put paid to the plan.

Knowledge check 8

What prompted the bomb plot of 1944?

Summary

When you have completed this section, you should have a thorough understanding of further developments in the Nazi control of Germany after 1933.

- The obstacles in the way of Hitler's complete political control of Germany, such as the democratic system of government, the president, the army, the radical wing of the SA and the traditional civil service.
- The entrenchment of Hitler's political control over German society through the stripping away of constitutional safeguards and liberties via measures such as the Enabling Act and the army's oath of allegiance.
- The transformation of the political system in Germany after 1933, for example the removal of the political opposition, the establishment of the dictatorship and the impact of the permanent state of emergency.
- The nature and extent of support for the Nazi regime after 1933: the different groups that offered positive support, compliance or acquiescence with the regime.
- The impact of propaganda, indoctrination and terror on the lives of the German people: persuasion through the mass media and direct force through the SS/Gestapo/SD complex.
- The nature and extent of opposition and resistance to the Nazi regime after 1933, such as the grumbling and minor dissent from the church and students, political activism from socialists and Communists and hostility from groups within the army.

■ The impact of Nazi racial, social and religious policies 1933–45

National Socialism was a movement of outsiders from within the Weimar Republic based on a radical, negative analysis of the existing system. But if the Nazis knew what they didn't want, what precisely did they want?

Until the assumption of power in 1933, the Nazis had existed in a virtual reality world of political opposition. They had no real understanding of what made Germany tick, or the practical realities of government. In opposition, it had not mattered to them that they were unable to present the German public with a coherent breakdown of their policies. Indeed, Hitler reasoned that there was no need to present a precise programme, because public opinion was not always influenced by logic or reason but was often driven by whims and prejudices.

Volksgemeinschaft

What appealed to the German people was the Nazi idea of an organic, harmonious national community, or Volksgemeinschaft, which had a common historical destiny and a common set of political beliefs. They believed that the Nazis were intent on a programme of complete social renewal, which would heal the wounds in society that had been created by the political mismanagement of the Weimar Republic. They would achieve a classless society.

However, it is more likely that the Nazis were using the notion of a national community to disguise the fact that they were intent on creating a:

- social solidarity based on the needs of the state, as opposed to the rights of the individual
- collective reaction against those who were deemed undeserving within society
- common set of enemies
- society where the state was to be the sole determinant of what was best for it
- a tidal wave of radical ideology, which would embed racism throughout society.

Hitler was able to get away with this strategy because he had latched onto a form of identity politics, where team, tribe, community and race mattered. He planned to use this not only to consolidate his power, but also to rebrand the German people in his own twisted image.

The Nazi regime did not want any dialogue with the German people, but instead demanded unity and compliance. The Nazis signalled a problem and their policies were designed to validate the steps they then took to deal with it. The harsh reality in Nazi Germany was that a person's role in society, their race, their ethnicity, their religion, their gender, and their physical and mental health all determined their life chances.

Nazi racial ideology

Those who believed that what Hitler wrote in *Mein Kampf* was a true statement of his views saw him as someone to be feared, because of the likely impact of his ideology on society. Others argued that his book was a product of passion and bitterness, and that once in power he would ditch his racial philosophy.

But was Hitler a man pursuing a defined ideological programme to its logical outcome or was he just a power-grabbing opportunist, with a confused mosaic of ideas?

The idea that the Nazis had an overarching ideology and philosophy which they faithfully put into practice is essentially flawed, because — for any party in power — the reality of government involves pragmatism, given that some things work in practice and others don't. But, even if ideas were not the essence of the regime or what underpinned its day-to-day operation, there was at least one enduring belief: social cohesion through a Volksgemeinschaft was to be based on the principles of racial unity and racial supremacy, and achieved by harnessing public grievances against minority groups. The results would be:

- explicit and violent nationalism
- that racial and ethnic minorities were made more vulnerable and there was sustained and pervasive vilification of Jewish people, with xenophobic discussions about their deportation
- disproportionate criminalisation of racial minorities
- lack of care, empathy or peripheral vision by a large proportion of the German people
- government-sponsored racial harassment.

Anti-Semitism in policy and practice

Germany was a society permeated by prejudices. Rhetoric does not always translate into policy but in this case it did, forced through by Hitler because of his own personal obsessions.

Anti-Semitism based on religious or social and economic prejudice pre-dated the Nazi Party. Hitler exploited it, using the tactic of blaming the country's problems on the alleged behaviour or practices of the Jewish community. By presenting the German people with something characterised as a threat to their identity and reinforcing it through negative propaganda, by playing on existing discontent and anger and channelling them in the direction of Jewish citizens, Hitler and the Nazis created a 'problem' to which a 'solution' would have to be found.

The Nazis were keen not to let their anti-Semitic policies prick the consciences of the German people. The strategy of blame meant that actions taken against Jewish people could be presented as defensive measures to protect the national community. This opened the door to the institutionalisation of anti-Semitism through state executive power. Racial policy in the period 1933–38 manifested itself in different forms, including personal abuse, physical violence, institutional prejudice and legislative discrimination.

Knowledge check 9

How was anti-Semitic propaganda delivered to the German people and put into practice by the regime?

The Nuremberg Laws: from random to legalised discrimination

The persecution of Jewish people was not a new phenomenon, but what was unprecedented were the lengths to which it was taken in the Third Reich. In Nazi ideology, a Jewish person was the complete antithesis of what it meant to be German, an arch enemy who was to be excluded and then removed from society.

Given that many of the rank and file within the Nazi Party were strongly committed to anti-Semitism it came as no surprise that there was an explosion of attacks against Jewish people and Jewish businesses following the 5 March election of 1933. These random acts of terror were succeeded by a more structured campaign of discrimination against what were potentially soft targets.

First Hitler organised a nationwide boycott of Jewish businesses and professions. In fact, the boycott was largely ignored and had minimal success. It was originally intended as indefinite, but in the face of opposition, Hitler decided to limit it to a single day, 1 April 1933 — saving face by retaining the option of reviving it at a later date if needed.

Knowledge check 10

Who was opposed to the boycott of Jewish businesses in 1933?

Meanwhile, hardliners such as Julius Streicher in *Der Stürmer* waged a negative campaign of racial profiling. This helped to foster a widespread passive anti-Semitism, but it did not fully convert the German public to the dynamic racism of Nazi ideology.

It became apparent to the militants that the only way to effectively enforce discriminatory policy was through systematic legislation. For their part, the civil servants who were to draft and process this legislation saw it as an acceptable transition to law and order from the lawless actions of the SA against Jewish people. But what they failed to acknowledge was that, beneath this cloak of legality, access to the law was being determined by racial status. Furthermore, anti-Semitic legislation, far from being coordinated from within the leadership, was being influenced in a more ad hoc manner by party extremists.

Knowledge check 11

What discriminatory laws were introduced during 1933?

From April to October 1933, a battery of laws was introduced to facilitate discrimination against Jewish people. Most German people acquiesced in the piecemeal process by which Jewish people were stripped of their status as fellow citizens and human beings in their own country.

Jewish people were systematically excluded and removed from the professional and cultural life of Germany. They were forced out of official positions in the civil service and judiciary, excluded completely from the media, and removed, by steps, from the medical, legal and teaching professions.

German blood and second-class citizenship

The bestial notion of racial blood differences was essential to Nazi ideology and its views of Nordic superiority. Jewish people were seen as polluters of German blood and contaminators of the Aryan race. Relationships between Jewish people and so-called Aryans had been a highly emotive subject for Nazi militants and they demanded a solution.

Aryan race The Herrenvolk, the superior or 'master' race.

The background to the Nuremberg Laws of 1935 was a revival of sporadic harassment and discrimination of Jewish people on a local level. The Nuremberg Laws provided additional legal validity and a new dimension to anti-Semitism because they laid the foundation for systematic racial discrimination.

Ironically, for some Jewish people the Nuremberg Laws possibly came as a relief, as it may have appeared that a limit had been set on anti-Semitic policy. This false impression might have been reinforced by the fact that anti-Semitism was toned down, for the sake of appearances, during the Berlin Olympics of 1936. However, the Nuremberg Laws meant that Jewish people were effectively second-class citizens, and any remaining rights could be removed piece by piece over the ensuing years.

Kristallnacht, 1938

If some German Jewish people felt that the parameters on discrimination had been set by the Nuremberg Laws, they were soon to be disappointed as anti-Semitism entered a new and more violent phase.

Kristallnacht, or the Night of Broken Glass, was presented in Nazi tabloids such as *Der Stürmer* as a spontaneous outburst of popular anger against the assassination of Ernst vom Rath, a diplomat in the German embassy in Paris. Herschel Grynszpan, a 17-year-old Polish Jewish person, had shot him in revenge for the recent expulsion of his parents from Germany.

The events that followed clearly revealed that discrimination had moved up a gear. Party radicals burned synagogues and looted property. It has been estimated that there were 91 deaths, and in the region of 30,000 Jewish men were arrested and detained in concentration camps.

Following Kristallnacht, the position of Jewish people deteriorated further as a number of discriminatory decrees were introduced. There was a clear intention to publicly humiliate and dispossess Jewish people, and there was a systematic attempt to reduce both the status and the livelihood of Jewish people, which included:

- the forced payment of a financial indemnity for the damage to property
- the forced surrender of gold, silver and precious jewellery
- Jewish pupils being expelled from schools, cinemas, universities, theatres and sports facilities
- Jewish people being banned from designated areas in cities
- bans on Jewish people visiting museums, theatres, concerts and swimming pools
- the withdrawal of driving licences
- enforced adoption of Jewish names such as Sara.

In addition:

- it became difficult for Jewish people to remain employers.
- From January 1939, Jewish people were not allowed to run retail shops or practise independent trades. Jewish employees in business could be dismissed at six weeks' notice.
- Jewish property was confiscated or 'Aryanised'.

With these last measures, the Nazis were effectively removing the Jewish community's means of material existence.

Knowledge check 12

What was the impact of the Nuremberg Laws on German Jewish people?

Another Nazi tabloid article, of 24 November 1938, gave an indication of the future for German Jewish people when it remarked that Jewish people would have to be reduced to dependence on crime. This would allow the state to take what it referred to as appropriate measures to protect law and order. Once again, the Nazis were using the pretext of upholding law and order to institute their own brand of lawlessness.

Exam tip

Focus upon the reaction of the German people to the events of Kristallnacht.

Emigration

The growing exclusion of Jewish people from all aspects of German life went on relentlessly. There was no doubt in the minds of many Jewish people that their prospects were very bleak if they remained in Germany.

The random acts of terror and the boycott of 1933 persuaded some 40,000 German Jewish people that the writing was on the wall about the direction of Nazi anti-Semitism and so they emigrated immediately. A steady exodus followed, and Kristallnacht and its aftermath pushed many more Jewish people into considering emigration as an option. In fact, by the outbreak of war in 1939, only about one-third of the original 500,000 German Jewish people remained in Germany.

Despite Reinhard Heydrich's goal of kicking all Jewish people out of Germany not everyone was inclined to leave, regarding themselves as patriotic Germans with a historical stake in the country. Even though they were effectively excluded from the economic life of the country, they still resisted the pressure from the Reich Central Office for Jewish Emigration and Eichmann's Reich Main Security Office in Berlin to emigrate.

For those who wanted to leave, however, it seemed that Nazi policy was insanely contradictory, because it was impoverishing Jewish people inside Germany while at the same time making them pay an emigration tax to secure passage out of the country. If they were destitute, how could they pay to leave? Others who were keen to go were further hampered by the fact that foreign countries placed obstacles in the way of accepting unlimited numbers of Jewish refugees.

The Nazi policy of forced emigration descended into farce with proposed plans to resettle Jewish people around the city of Lublin in Poland and later on the island of Madagascar. Heydrich referred to these external proposals as the territorial final solution to the Jewish question.

Anti-Semitism had been declared openly in the 25-point programme of National Socialism of 1920 and in the poisonous *Mein Kampf* of 1925. It had become enshrined in the Nuremberg Laws of 1935, and now it had been clearly exposed in the events of Kristallnacht in 1938. It can therefore be argued that Hitler's anti-Semitism was becoming transformed into policy and practice as the opportunities presented themselves.

Policies towards asocials

Social regulation and negative eugenics

Asocial was a very flexible term used by the Nazis for all those who fell outside the social norms of the Nazi national community, including beggars, habitual criminals, those considered 'work-shy', alcoholics, sex workers and even juvenile delinquents.

These groups were seen as a burden on social welfare, a threat to public order, or both. They were regarded by the Nazis as a product of criminal biology. Individuals with specific social problems counted for nothing in National Socialist ideology when the defence of the national community was at stake.

As far as the Nazis were concerned, the restoration of racial purity through eugenics was a vital step in the creation of the Volksgemeinschaft. Any actions taken by the government in relation to social policy, therefore, were always considered in terms of whether they benefited the race and the nation. For example, homosexual people were treated as asocials because they did not measure up to Nazi expectations of typical German family life, as were Sinti and Roma people, who did not conform to the Aryan stereotype.

Compulsory sterilisation and selective euthanasia

In 1934, the Nazis introduced the Law for the Prevention of Hereditarily Diseased Offspring, which authorised the compulsory sterilisation of all those people who were identified as suffering from one of a range of often vaguely identified hereditary illnesses. These people were deemed socially inefficient.

The Nazis became responsible for murdering large numbers of men, women and children with disabilities or who were mentally ill. They were aided and abetted by nurses and doctors who believed in the moral probity of what they were doing.

By 1941 over 70,000 adult patients had been murdered by the Aktion T4 programme. Operating from a suburban villa at Tiergartenstrasse 4, Berlin, a team of 'expert' assessors identified and selected their victims. A specially created Community Patients Transport Service removed them to one of six asylums, where they were killed. It started in 1939 and was the first Nazi programme to use poison gas to kill its victims. By 1945, 6,000 babies, children and teenagers had also been murdered. The victims had been judged to be unworthy of life, or as it appeared in some school textbooks, useless eaters.

Suspicions were aroused when deaths at psychiatric institutions became mysteriously common. In order to stem the growing public outcry, the Nazis officially ended the programme in August 1941. But the murder of children continued, less state-centralised but state-encouraged.

It is also claimed that more children died after the T4 programme ended than during it, although the victims were not gassed but died of starvation or from lethal injections.

In addition, up to 50,000 people were selected from concentration camps on the grounds of mental illness, physical incapacity or racial origin under a separate programme with the code 14F13, the reference number for the Inspector of Concentration Camps.

Social policies

Social policy is essentially about establishing boundaries within society. While the implementation of policies is important, holding them in place is the key to maintaining order, discipline and general conformity within society.

Aktion T4 programme
The Nazi euthanasia programme, directed against people with disabilities and some hereditary and mental illnesses. It began in 1939 and was the first time the Nazis used poison gas (among other methods) to murder their victims.

Exam tip

Nazi measures against racial and social minorities became more extreme as time went on.

The Nazis took social policy a step further in attempting to control people's behaviour. They were seeking to secure uniformity of thought and action within German society. No social group was to be overlooked and nothing was to be left to chance.

Young people

Any society should aim to encourage young people to develop lively enquiring minds and attributes such as perspective, perceptiveness and self-perception.

This was not the case in the Third Reich, where closing minds and drawing young people into the Nazi ethos was the main aim. The Nazis wanted to establish a race of doers, not thinkers. Learning was to be based on the principle of whether it was in the spirit of National Socialism, not on whether it was true and accurate. Textbooks were rewritten to promote the ideas of Germany's greatness and Aryan superiority. Teachers had to join the National Socialist Teachers League, and Jewish teachers were sacked.

In order to develop resilience to propaganda, you first need to learn how to recognise it. In Nazi Germany, however, the Nazis were keen to prevent young people from acquiring the tools to do this. This meant that young people may have been more susceptible to Hitler's appeal than the older generation, who were more likely to be set in their ways, with pre-established notions of class and loyalty.

Between 1933 and 1945, three separate age groups passed through the adolescent years of 14 to 18 and each group had its own distinctive experiences.

■ The adolescents in the period 1933–36 had experienced the economic crisis of the early 1930s and were quite receptive to the ideas of Volksgemeinschaft and the benefits of the rearmament programme. They were in the front line for incorporation within the Hitler Youth.
■ The young people of the period 1936–39 bore the stamp of National Socialism, having gone through the Hitler Youth programme. Life for them seemed predictable and devoid of an alternative route. The Hitler Youth presented itself as a sanctuary from the traditional authority of home and school.
■ In the years 1939–45, the war reduced the Hitler Youth's capacity to provide leisure activities and members had to perform war duties such as helping in rescue attempts after air raids. Towards the very end of the war, some boys as young as 14 and 15 had to fight the invading Allies.

Table 4 shows the contrasting reactions of young people to Nazi ideas and imperatives.

Table 4 Young people's responses to Nazi ideology

Nazi ideology	Positive reactions	Negative reactions
A new role for young people in Nazi Germany	National Socialism claimed to replace an outworn civilisation with a new one and this gave hope to some of Germany's youth. It implied that the older generation would be replaced by the new.	Promises of well-paid jobs for young people within the administration and the party apparatus failed to materialise. Opposition came through youth subcultures and later through groups such as the Edelweiss Pirates. There was a reaction against the Hitler Youth. Almost 25% of young people were able to avoid membership of the Hitler Youth by 1939.
Becoming part of a new society	Young people were attracted by the dynamism and novelty of the movement, and also by the gross simplifications that were presented to them. The Nazis appealed to the crowd instinct. The atmosphere of unity (against common enemies) was attractive to many.	Some became irritated by the loss of personal freedom and by the authority over them claimed by Hitler Youth patrols of the same age. Not all young people were prepared to be shaped according to a National Socialist blueprint.
Embracing nationalist ideology	The emphasis on patriotism found a resonance with many young people. Hitler was calling on young people to share in a moral crusade about duty, faith and honour. It appealed to the restless spirit of young people and actively engaged them in Hitler's expansionist ambitions.	The education system was geared to promoting a nationalist and racist ideology. Some children became bored by the revised curriculum in schools. They were starved of reading materials and free discussions. Alternative ideas were never explored.
Obedience to the state above all else	Some children whose parents did not support the Nazis rebelled against, or even denounced, their parents with the encouragement of schools and the Hitler Youth. Some young people liked the enhanced sense of comradeship and kinship that they felt in the Hitler Youth. The movement created a 'we who belong' consciousness. It also provided some with their first access to leisure activities.	Young people often selected from other competing sources of information and values, for example from the church or from literature, which they hid away. The more powers the Hitler Youth acquired, the more it led to a rebellious counter-reaction from some adolescents. Young people began to turn away from the prescribed leisure activities of the Hitler Youth, preferring their own unregimented style or seeking out alternative lifestyles. Some (mostly middle-class teenagers) joined groups like Swing Youth and Jazz Youth, and danced to banned jazz music in clubs.
The Nazi philosophy of education	Some young people enjoyed the Nazis' rejection of intellectual thinking. There was no pressure to be clever — rather, there was deep contempt for learning. The promotion of sport in schools matched this anti-academic ethos.	Creativity and the potential for independent thought were snuffed out. Young people found themselves in an educational straitjacket as genuine learning was replaced by a Nazi-controlled curriculum. Some young people became resentful of the regimentation and petty restrictions imposed by the regime through schools and the Hitler Youth organisation.
Conformity to the Nazi ideal	Some young people were impressed with the harsh line against non-conformity to the Nazi ideal. Why would anyone want to be different unless they were enemies of the German people?	Every game, every piece of art and craft, every experience was measured against a preconceived Nazi ideal.

Women

The 1919 constitution of the Weimar Republic had given women the vote and proclaimed their equality with men. It would have appeared that the liberation of German women from the fetters of the Wilhelmine period was well underway.

- Educational opportunities had greatly improved.
- The world of business and the professions had opened up to women.
- In the 1920s, 11 million women were working full-time.
- By the end of the Weimar period, one-third of the total labour force was female.

However, the reality was somewhat different, and the advances in the status of women were more apparent than real.

- Most women remained in manual work, domestic service or white-collar jobs.
- A third of all women were unpaid helpers on farms or in family businesses.
- Prospects for promotion were slim.
- Most female workers were unmarried, with married women tending to remain at home.

In the light of these experiences it could be argued that despite some progress, for most women in Germany, employment was nothing more than a stage between school and marriage.

Nazi ideology was well placed to take advantage of this, because it fundamentally opposed the social and economic emancipation of women. Nazi policy was repressive and reactionary, founded on the view that men and women had distinct roles to play within society based on their natural differences. The Nazis were keen to de-feminise the entire public service, and their policies resulted in the displacement of women from public life.

This policy has been referred to by some as a kind of secondary racism because it led to female subordination. However, whether all German women viewed their new role in these terms is open to question, for while some were angered by their removal from many sectors of employment, especially the professions, others were attracted to Hitler's idealised image of motherhood.

Promotion of motherhood

The regime embarked on a series of measures to encourage women to leave the professions and to marry and produce children, with seemingly very successful results. Looking at the statistical evidence, as shown in Table 5 below, it would appear that Nazi ideology had succeeded in what was characterised as a battle for births.

Table 5 Numbers of marriages and births in four years between 1932 and 1939

Year	Marriages	Births
1932	516,793	993,126
1935	651,435	1,263,976
1938	645,062	1,348,534
1939	772,106	1,407,490

Exam tip

Statistical evidence relating to dictatorships should always be treated with caution and never considered in isolation. As a historian you will need to consider other sociological, personal and psychological factors that influenced increased marriage and birth rates in Nazi Germany.

However, the increased birth rate was not completely the result of an ideological drive but was policy driven, as:

- abortion was outlawed
- birth control clinics were closed
- access to contraceptives was restricted
- financial incentives were given to women to marry and have children
- greater welfare support was given to mothers
- symbolic rewards were offered such as the Mother's Cross.

Hitler was, of course, in a position to impose upon women his vision of what he saw as their role in building the Thousand-Year Reich.

Taking women out of the workforce

Nazi policies towards women in the workplace included the following.

- Married women were dismissed from their jobs.
- A purge of the legal profession culminated in 1936 with a ban on women working as judges, prosecutors or assessors.
- The number of female teachers at elementary schools was reduced, and there was a curtailment in the admission of women to universities.
- Interest-free loans were provided to women who were prepared to give up their jobs and get married or where there was double employment within the family.

Women were to be the bearers of children to build the future of the Third Reich and perpetuate Nazi culture. This message was to be reinforced through Nazi women's organisations such as the National Socialist Women's League, the NS-Frauenschaft.

Reinforcing the Nazi role

The task of the Nazi women's organisations was to encourage women in their 'natural' role through cultural, educational and social programmes. The NS-Frauenschaft was a key channel of Nazi propaganda, both through its activities and its magazine, the *NS-Frauen-Warte*. Many women were easily seduced by Nazi rhetoric, which exalted their role, with its responsibility for Kinder, Küche, Kirche. There is little evidence that many women at this time objected to the official attitude: even leading figures in the pre-1933 women's movement came to support the Nazis.

The role of women as supportive wives and mothers was portrayed as an essential ingredient in making a stable society, and their willing sacrifice of individual freedom as being necessary for the greater national good. But it led to unprecedented state interference in their private lives. The Nazi state showed little interest in single women other than in their potential to marry and produce children. In schools there were compulsory courses for girls in biology and domestic science, racial awareness and an increased emphasis on physical fitness.

Unmarried mothers, who were stigmatised at this time in most European countries, were given an enhanced status through the Lebensborn campaign. The procreation of children of 'good blood' was so valued that the image of an unmarried mother with an illegitimate child was recast for the good of the German community. Racially perfect men drawn from the SS were, according to Himmler, to become conception assistants.

Knowledge check 13

What was the Mother's Cross?

Kinder, Küche, Kirche Children, kitchen, church: these were meant to be the chief occupations and concerns of women in the Third Reich.

Lebensborn The spring of life: a state-sponsored programme to safeguard the propagation of children of pure German blood, regardless of marriage bonds.

It ultimately led to the collusion of many German women with the ideology of a racist state. This has led to a re-evaluation of the role of women within the Third Reich, and they are no longer seen as simply passive victims of an obscene political system. However, it should also be emphasised that racially 'inferior' women or asocial women unequivocally endured a catalogue of human rights abuses such as sterilisation at the hands of the Nazi state.

Reintroducing women into the workforce

Despite the prestige bestowed on women as wives and mothers, this ideological position was later undermined by the consequences of progressive industrialisation and an expanding economy. This led to the social and economic mobilisation of women, especially during the Second World War. The number of working women increased from 4.52 million to 5.2 million between 1936 and 1938 alone.

By May 1939, 14.6 million women had been mobilised as part of the civilian workforce. By September 1944 this had increased to 14.9 million. As the regime moved towards war, women had to combine the roles of mother, housewife, party member and industrial worker. The military discipline in factories exposed women, perhaps for the first time, to the full force of undisguised state power.

As the demands on women increased, no doubt some women met the realities of Nazi policy with silent anger and resignation rather than with enthusiastic patriotic support.

No doubt, while some women openly collaborated with the Third Reich others did not. In the final analysis, however, many German women were actively involved in the Nazi movement and played an equal role in helping to make war and its consequences possible.

Workers

The Nazis knew that if the entire workforce turned against the system the economy would collapse. Therefore, in order to secure economic growth and social stability Hitler was clearly aware of the necessity of binding the workers to the Nazi state. He wanted a strong, unified German nation in which the workers would have a respected but subordinate role.

However, despite rhetoric that extolled the nobility of labour and the equality of all true German people the status of German workers did not really improve. Hitler offered them work and better wages and conditions, but without trade unions and the legal ability to strike it was unlikely that workers could secure those benefits indefinitely. The national average working week lasted 47 hours in 1939 rising to 52 by 1943. Some workers accepted the increase because they felt that it was their patriotic duty to respond to Nazi priorities. Other workers, however, were simply driven by the need to earn money.

The Nazis created an idealised image of work, but the response of the workers was not always positive. Table 6 shows some of the different impacts of particular policies on workers.

Table 6 Positive and negative impacts of Nazi workplace and employment policies

Nazi policy	Positive impact on workers	Negative impact on workers
The banning of trade unions	The loss of trade union power may have had less of a psychological impact on younger workers who had not experienced belonging to a union.	Workers were pressed into entering the German Labour Front, a Nazi-directed trade union really for the organisation of labour. To the older workers this was an infringement of liberty.
Workforce organisations	Negative reactions against rearmament were offset by incentives such as higher wages, cultural events, housing projects, social support networks and the funding of the Strength Through Joy outings and activities. With these measures the Nazis appeared to be doing something tangible for the workers.	Wages may have increased but this was mainly the result of an increase in working hours. Measures ostensibly designed to improve the health and well-being of the workers also benefited the state through improved productivity. Leisure activities provided by Strength Through Joy gave the state further opportunities to regulate people's social life and inculcate Nazi values. The workers began to be less impressed by national community propaganda. There were strikes in 1936.
Reducing unemployment	Having a secure job was more important to many people than the right to free collective bargaining or whether wages were higher or lower. Workers had fresh memories of the misery of unemployment during the Depression. Many people simply wanted to earn and get on with life. If this was the sole gift that National Socialism could offer them, so be it.	Workers had limited freedom of occupational choice and limited freedom of movement. No doubt many workers remained sceptical if not alienated from the regime as they witnessed business owners making handsome gains from the boom in German industry.
Preparing the economy for war	The working classes were not enthusiastic about the outbreak of war in 1939, but the large majority of Germany's workers did what was expected of them right up to the bitter end. The massive majority of German workers did not challenge the framework of the Hitler state.	Illness, absenteeism and accidents doubled between 1936 and 1939. Without organised representation, workers had little means of either improving their conditions or protesting about them. Feelings of isolation and vulnerability could only be expressed in a kind of grumbling apathy.

Policies towards religion

In some respects the Christian churches were both compliant and complicit in enabling the Nazis to carry out their policies, even though they were the only institutions allowed to retain organisational autonomy in Nazi Germany. As such, they had the potential to speak out against National Socialism through any church in the land.

The Third Reich offered a different road to 'salvation' through the national community, with a new and perfect Aryan order to replace the old. Consequently, the Nazis saw religion as something of an unwanted guest. They would try in the short term to carve out an acceptable space for religion while maintaining the racial purity of the national community through a programme of state-sponsored eugenics and indoctrinatory education. In truth the writing was already on the wall for the status of religion within Nazi society. Indeed, the state's intentions became clear in 1939, in the captured Polish territories, where it established a new order free of churches.

Hitler admired the church for its techniques of mass manipulation, but not for its Christian message. Although in the early Nazi programmes he referred to positive Christianity, this was a very grey area. In 1933 he spoke privately of being either a Christian or a German and ultimately he wanted to suppress the church as an institution altogether. However, the Nazis were conscious that a conflict with the churches would alienate many people, so initially they were prepared to compromise.

The churches realised there were bound to be clashes with the state over its social and religious policies, given their own responsibility to object to any attempt to undermine Christian principles. However, they also knew that it would serve the interests of the church to limit the nature and extent of those clashes. On some occasions, therefore, the churches favoured compliance over conflict.

The Catholic church

The Catholic church had been against the liberal values of Weimar on education, abortion and civil marriages, which offended core Catholic beliefs. It shared the Nazis' view of the role of women and the importance of family, and supported their attacks on communism and socialism. The Catholic Centre Party helped to secure the passage of the Enabling Act in 1933, thus paving the way for Hitler to assume dictatorial powers. And there were some churchmen, like Cardinal von Faulhaber, who collaborated with the regime to the end, despite some reservations about its excesses.

In spite of this, the Catholic church posed a potential threat to the regime. Unlike political groups, it could not be abolished or incorporated into the regime, and its teachings were essentially at odds with key Nazi policies and practices. In addition, Catholics owed allegiance to the Pope, which implied a check on Hitler's authority, and the Catholic church had an existence that was independent of the regime. It was internationally based and had its own network of schools, clubs and societies and — until 1936, when they were disbanded — youth groups.

Nazi handling of the Catholic church

- The Nazi regime wanted the Catholic church to legitimise it, and in 1933 a Concordat was signed between the German government and the Vatican. The Concordat guaranteed the rights of the Catholic church in Germany. However, as far as the Nazis were concerned, this was only a tactical agreement. They had no real intention of abiding by the terms of the Concordat and soon violated it.
- In 1935, Hanns Kerrl was appointed Reich minister for church affairs to deal with church resistance groups and to curb their activities through legally binding ordinances.
- The Nazis were able to use the Catholic church's fear of communism to limit criticism of other Nazi policies.
- While there appeared to be accommodation with the church hierarchy, the regime carried out surveillance, mass punishment and persecution of some clergy at the grassroots level. More than 200 priests were accused of financial and sexual misbehaviour. Public immorality trials were used to discredit the clergy.
- The government's response to opposition from the clergy after 1939 was to call them up for war service.

Concordat The Reichskonkordat was a treaty negotiated between the Vatican and the German government and signed on 20 July 1933. Among other terms, it limited the political activity of Catholic clergy.

- They attempted to undermine the church with the creation of the German Faith Movement. This essentially non-Christian religion attacked the sacred tenets of Christianity.
- The Nazis subverted the Concordat with the Catholic church through the creation of organisations such as the Cross and Eagle League, and the working group of Catholic German people, who sought to disseminate Nazi values.

Clashes

- Throughout the 1930s Catholics organised local grassroots campaigns against Nazi attempts to ban the display of crucifixes in Catholic schools and replace them with portraits of the Führer.
- In 1937 Pope Pius XI wrote in a papal encyclical 'with deep anxiety' about the interference of the state in education but with no effect.
- In 1941 Bishop Galen preached against the Nazis' euthanasia programme and there was opposition to sterilisation. The clamour became so loud that Hitler had to order the temporary end of euthanasia actions. However, once again we should consider that the Catholic church spoke out against aspects of racial policy that might affect German families, such as eugenics and euthanasia, but not essentially against Nazi ideology.

The Protestant church

The Protestant church had a long history of obedience to political authority. It detested socialism and identified with the Nazi emphasis on moral values and the family. This stood in stark contrast to the materialism that they associated with the Weimar Republic.

The Protestant church also supported the restoration of national pride. There was even a group within the church calling themselves the 'German Christians', who gave full support to the regime and came to be labelled the 'SA of the church'. They believed that Christianity was essentially a Nordic religion which had been corrupted by Jewish influences, so that German people had a divine right to solve the 'Jewish problem'. Although there were notable individuals who opposed the regime, the Protestant church in general sought to avoid conflict without endorsing all aspects of Nazi policies.

Nazi handling of the Protestant church

The Nazis wanted a centralised and unified Protestant church, and so Hitler appointed Ludwig Müller as national bishop of the newly created Nazi Reich church, which combined Christian beliefs with racism, anti-clericalism and Führer worship.

Clashes

- Protestants cherished a tradition of religious independence, which implied a challenge to Hitler's authority.
- The drive to Nazify the church led to a strong response from a dissident group called the Pastors' Emergency League (which evolved into the Confessing church), led by Pastor Martin Niemöller, who was arrested and placed in 'protective custody' in Sachsenhausen and Dachau concentration camps. Niemöller was eventually determined to resist the advance of any Nazi-tainted Christianity.

- Another key founding member of the Confessing church was Dietrich Bonhoeffer. Unlike Niemöller, who had initially welcomed Hitler's rise to power, Bonhoeffer was thoroughly opposed to the regime and quickly spoke out against it. He worked for the German resistance movement during the war and was executed in Flossenbürg concentration camp in 1945.
- About 800 pastors of the Confessing church were arrested and sent to concentration camps.

The reaction of the German churches: conflict or compliance?

- The churches mainly displayed passive acquiescence towards National Socialism. They were arguably keener to uphold the institutions of Christianity than its principles. They focused on providing pastoral and spiritual comfort rather than on fulfilling their greater moral duty to society.
- Some of the more radical theologians accepted some of the many negative eugenic policies such as compulsory sterilisation.
- The church authorities would not openly endanger their relationship with the Nazi regime, so protest was left to conscientious individuals.
- We have the impression that as long as they could retain their independence, a large number of Protestants were content to go along with the regime.
- The church in general accepted aspects of Hitler's solution of the 'Jewish question' and the euthanasia programme.
- Some members and clergy from both churches shared the anti-Semitism of the regime, which included myths of Jewish treachery and deicide. They also supported the regime's anti-Communist position.
- Pius XII has been branded by some as 'Hitler's Pope'. As the Papal Nuncio in Berlin, he had developed affections for Germany which some say later blinded him to the atrocities carried out in Germany's name. He has also been accused of anti-Semitism. However, apologists for Pius XII have argued that his policy of unprovocative practical help (instructing the clergy to provide aid and sanctuary) saved more lives than would have been achieved through open verbal condemnation of Nazi policy.
- Opposition from within the churches gave them a new inner vitality and provoked a Christian solidarity, which was a distinctive feature of German opposition and allowed the church to recover lost ground. There was no significant decline in church membership in the 1930s, indicating that the Nazis had failed to break the ties between the people and religion within the national community.

Exam tip

There is a danger of misconstruing the role of the church in Nazi Germany. You should resist the temptation to become a hanging judge on the institution as a whole without considering the reactions of individual clergy towards the excesses of National Socialism.

The degree of Volksgemeinschaft

The Nazis were seeking a radical ideological transformation of German society. Whether or not this resulted in a new social mentality and a new social order in Germany is open to question. It is important to evaluate changes in German society within the context of whether they were positive, progressive or morally defensible. Judged against these criteria, it is not difficult to reach the conclusion that the Nazi Volksgemeinschaft had only a destructive impact on German society. A movement that wanted to create a society based upon race, eugenics, social efficiency and ideological conformity could surely never have resulted in a positive outcome for the German people.

It is claimed that Hitler once stated that 'The Nazi social programme was a great landscape painted on the background of our stage'. This would suggest that the Volksgemeinschaft was less a serious declaration of intent and more a propaganda exercise.

Since the philosophy of National Socialism was a mass of contradictions it was impossible to create a constructive new social order from within it. Furthermore, Hitler saw society as little more than an instrument for achieving his expansionist aims in foreign policy. War was the end process of a reconstruction of society built on a platform of racial purification.

There were some profound and significant changes in the period 1933–45, which were mainly achieved at the expense of the German people.

- Pre-existing nationalist and anti-Semitic prejudices in German education were greatly increased, with the curriculum and textbooks altered to inculcate Nazi ideology, and the sacking of Jewish teachers.
- National Socialism broke through existing solidarities and fostered extreme racial and social intolerance. The operation of a police state and the policy of encouraging people to inform on friends and neighbours created a fractured society.
- The reality of 'classless' German society meant that the workers were more or less enslaved. The position of the employers was strengthened and working-class organisations were destroyed. Trade unions had been abolished so that the workers had no rights to free collective bargaining. This meant that they had to work harder and for longer.
- 'Blood and soil' ideology existed side by side with advanced industrialisation, which drew the rural population from the countryside to the towns.
- Nazi policy towards women was contradictory and confused. The enhanced status of family life was a fiction, given that within the Hitler Youth, children were encouraged to inform on their parents if they thought they were disloyal to the regime.

Summary

When you have completed this section, you should have a thorough knowledge of the impact of Nazi racial, social and religious policies in the period 1933–45.

- The importance in Nazi ideology of the idea of the racial supremacy of the German people, the concept of the Aryan race and the inferiority of racial minorities; how race and society became inseparable with the desire to create a new social order, the Volksgemeinschaft.
- The escalation in the measures taken against minorities, especially the increase in persecution of Jewish people, but also of the so-called asocials.
- The extent to which young people were controlled and indoctrinated through education and the Hitler Youth programme.
- The changing role and status of different groups such as women and workers.
- The Nazi attempt to free the German people from the influence of the church, and the creation of the Nazi Reich church.

■ The effectiveness of Nazi economic policy 1933–45

The performance of the economy under the Nazis

In any society, economic priorities are determined both by the preferences of government leaders and the constraints that they are working under. This means that politics and economics are inextricably interwoven. Economic policy is the result of a complex process, which should involve the identification of priorities:

■ through acute oversight
■ with appropriate planning in terms of time-scale and funding
■ with reinforcement by effective legislation and regulation.

Nazi economic policy, however, was not consistently based upon these key processes. This has led to the widely accepted belief that Nazi economic policy was based on pragmatic solutions to the political and ideological priorities of the Third Reich.

In the absence of any smooth functioning system of planning and policy making, Hitler instead counted on developing a 'new social and economic consciousness' within the national community. He believed that the willpower of the German people would resolve any economic problems through a spirit of national self-assertion, and that it would all turn out well in the end. Economic awareness, as far as the Nazis were concerned, was the result of a shared experience in the process of economic change and development. How would this translate into practice?

The recovery and Schacht, 1933–36

The German people had high expectations of the Nazis when they came to power. But, despite the ambitious campaign pledges of 'work and bread' and the semi-socialist slogans of the 25-point programme, Hitler did not have a coherent economic policy when he became chancellor in 1933.

The German economy was clearly in need of serious attention. The collapse of the international trading system and the return to world-wide protectionism following the Depression confirmed to the Nazis that the old liberal economic order had failed and that a new order was necessary.

Of course, any new government should try to resolve the economic difficulties it inherits. However, this was not entirely the case with the new Nazi regime. It had a set of political and economic priorities which meant that the solutions it adopted would be designed to steer Germany in a different direction. Furthermore, there were no formal constraints on Hitler's handling of the economy, especially after 1934, because of the nature of his dictatorship. This meant that his approach was often based on finding ad hoc solutions, which was not a sound economic principle. Therefore, the ideology and methods of the Nazi regime arguably limited the capacity of the government to find effective solutions to the economic problems it faced.

Knowledge check 14

Find some examples of semi-socialist slogans from the 25-point programme.

Protectionism An attempt to protect the home economy by restriction of free trade and the imposition of import duties.

Economic nationalism and the battle against unemployment

In 1933, Germany had mass unemployment, an impoverished rural sector, declining trade, balance of payment difficulties and a credit system on the brink of collapse. The Nazi regime chose to use a combination of economic interventions in order to enforce economic nationalism. This was an extension of National Socialist ideology, which emphasised the importance of a national effort at renewal built on the principle of individual self-sacrifice. It was intended to improve the performance of the German economy and to make Germany self-sufficient in food and essential raw materials.

The main priority in the period 1933–36, in this first Four-Year Plan, was to maintain the support of the population and to revive the military and industrial power of Germany through investment, regulation, incentives and persuasion.

Investment

Money was part of the key to an economic recovery. This was facilitated by the state through its new financial expert Hjalmar Schacht. His appointment as president of the Reichsbank in 1933 and economics minister in 1934 indicated that the Nazis were not engaged in any wild economic experiments. In fact, Schacht's appointment was a gesture of reassurance to big business. He was prepared to extend to the government unlimited credit. Deficit financing was built on the principle that governments should increase and not cut expenditure to lift an economy out of a recession.

Job-creation schemes

Job-creation schemes rapidly reduced unemployment: by the end of 1938 less than 500,000 people were unemployed. Table 7 shows the falls in the numbers and percentage of German people unemployed through the 1930s. But Schacht only expanded the work of previous governments in the provision of public work schemes. The Nazis had not changed the basic strategy, but were attempting to make it more effective.

Table 7 The superficial results of the battle for labour

Year (January figures)	Number unemployed	Percentage of the workforce unemployed
1933	6 million	25.9
1934	3.3 million	13.9
1935	2.9 million	10.3
1936	2.5 million	7.4
1937	1.8 million	4.1
1938	1.05 million	1.9
1939	300,000	0.5

Regulation

The banning of trade unions

As there was now a national community, there was no need for divisive pressure groups such as trade unions — this was how Nazi propaganda sold the case to German workers. In reality, the unions, with their affiliation to the SPD, were a potential source of opposition. On 2 May 1933 the SS forcibly shut down the unions, arrested their leaders and confiscated their assets. The industrialists had no objections, hoping that the absence of trade unions would lead to increases in production.

The German Labour Front

The German Labour Front, DAF, was meant to represent both workers and employers. For workers, it was really a toothless substitute for trade unions, as they no longer had any means of bargaining. Strikes were effectively outlawed from 1933.

To win what the Nazis referred to as the battle of labour between 1933 and 1935, it was important that the DAF attempted to appeal to a sense of national pride and a strong work ethic in order to increase productivity. This was done partly through the incentives offered by the Strength Through Joy programme (see under Incentives, below). However, the DAF was also designed to maintain control over the workforce, acting as a barometer of shop-floor attitudes.

The New Plan

Schacht's New Plan of 1934 was intended to promote exports, reduce imports, strengthen the currency and establish bilateral agreements with countries in the Balkans and South America, which were rich in raw materials.

His strategy was aimed at establishing an economic balance that would place Germany on a path to self-sufficiency. The German countryside was scoured for raw materials, and experiments in the production of synthetic products, such as petrol from coal, began. The New Plan is sometimes seen as a first step in the move towards total war because Germany was building an economic revival from its own resources.

Economic regimentation

This came in the form of wage controls and restrictions on changing jobs, which amounted to a curtailment on workers' freedom of movement and vocational choices.

The Reich Inherited Farm Law

The fear of indebtedness was lifted from thousands of German farmers by the Reich Inherited Farm Law of September 1933. It gave protection to farmers against the risk of foreclosure, but drastically reduced the ability of small farmers to dispose of their property or share it among their heirs. Also, rural migration to the towns led to a labour shortage in the countryside, which made farm maintenance more difficult and led to a demand for increased wages. Production and profit lapsed as a result.

Incentives

By 1938, the state was investing five times as much money as in 1933, but the traditional capitalist structure was also utilised. There developed a mixture of state and private investment, and tax concessions were provided to industry in order to finance the state-directed expansion.

Nazi economic priorities also wore the benevolent mask of socialism. The Kraft durch Freude (Strength Through Joy) programme was intended to offer less well-paid workers a share in activities that had only been affordable to the better-off. The benefits obtained through KdF included a variety of adult education, health and leisure programmes, and workplace access to facilities such as libraries, swimming pools, gyms and other sports facilities. KdF also organised visits to concerts and films, and provided subsidised holidays, cruises and day trips. The less benevolent aspects of these incentives were that they were intended to build public loyalty to the regime, and that they tightened the state's grip on people's activities by exerting more control over what they did in their spare time.

The Schönheit der Arbeit (Beauty of Labour) scheme advocated the improvement of the working environment, for example through noise reduction and improvements in air quality and cleanliness, along with better facilities such as changing rooms and lockers. In 1934, the government offered marriage loans, which were part of a wider plan to boost consumer demand. Schacht used deficit financing as a means of encouraging greater domestic demand because it increased the amount of money available for public expenditure in industries. He raised finance by the introduction of Mefo Bills, which were essentially credit notes that could be cashed in with interest after five years.

Persuasion

Propaganda convinced the German workers that they were better off because of regular employment and a slight rise in living standards. They now had an enhanced position within the national community. However, the price paid included the loss of the right to free collective bargaining and longer hours of work. The average working week increased from 42.9 hours in 1933 to 47 by the beginning of 1939. Real wages trailed behind because of inflation.

A defence economy

Of course, war and a policy of expansionism were a further extension of economic nationalism, so that even the recovery was instigated with one eye on military expansion. The whole of the economy in peacetime was ultimately being targeted to the needs of a future war. Rearmament would help to reduce unemployment. Military strength would have to be linked to material and technological advancement and the transport system would need to be put in order and expanded.

Autobahns would help to improve Germany's infrastructure and were a visual symbol of national progress and unity. These improvements in infrastructure would later facilitate the mobilisation for war.

In an ideal world, governments should ensure that their economic policies create mutual gains and that the economic outcomes are fair for all sectors of society. Unfair economic outcomes are usually the result of either the unfeasibility of the original policy, the interests of powerful groups or the failure of governments to implement public policy. In the case of the Third Reich probably all three scenarios applied. German industry may have been booming, and the majority of the population benefited, but not all benefited equally, and some lost out. The recovery was not equal across all sectors, and only in 1935 did unemployment come down to 1928 levels.

Rearmament, the second Four-Year Plan and Göring

In 1936, there was a significant change in emphasis in the management of the economy. Hitler wanted to turn Germany into an economic and military superpower before the rest of the world could catch up. He needed a resilient economic infrastructure to accommodate the increased military expenditure and this meant:

- the development of the industrial and raw materials sectors
- the production of substitute products in case of blockade
- the training of the workforce in easily transferable skills
- the development of an adequate food base and war rationing.

Autobahns Motorways: a programme of motorway building began in 1933, creating employment and also serving as a symbol of German unity, in that the expansion of roads made it easier for German people to travel around the country and appreciate its beauty.

Knowledge check 16

Who gained and who lost out in the economic recovery?

On 18 October 1936, Hitler announced the second Four-Year Plan, with Hermann Göring in charge. Göring set about establishing an organisation made up of six departments to facilitate the operation of the plan. Its aim was to make the German armed forces ready for war in four years. To achieve this, there was a drive for self-sufficiency in agriculture and industry through increased production and the development of synthetic products. Nazi controls over industry became much tighter.

How effective was the second Four-Year Plan?

Hitler's plan was a major turning point both in the development of the German economy in general and the build-up of military preparations in particular. However, it was more of an indicative timetable than a firm plan with schedules and deadlines, and the result was that by 1939, the Germany economy was still in transition from a peace to a war economy — and therefore not ready for war. Nor had the goal of agricultural self-sufficiency been achieved.

The second Four-Year Plan undermined Schacht to the extent that he resigned in November 1937. Between 1933 and 1936, he had maintained a delicate balance between consumer and military needs. He had argued that if the country was buying more than it could pay for then it needed to economise. To Schacht this meant cutting back on rearmament — but this was not compatible with Hitler's aims. Schacht had also regarded synthetic production as essentially un-economic and felt that it was far cheaper to import. The production of synthetic fuel only ever covered 18% of demand.

Göring, in his attempt to drive Germany forward as a military and industrial power, also needed to balance the needs of the consumer against those of the military. But the focus on rearmament meant that the regime had to control consumer demand. Göring therefore pushed for a reduction in public consumption, using the propaganda slogan guns not butter.

However, the regime had to tread carefully, because the imposition of an austerity programme ran the risk of depressing living standards, which could bring about social unrest. Raising taxes was also out of the question because of the potentially damaging effects for the stability of the government.

In addition, a coherent strategy for rearmament had failed to emerge because of:
- the inadequacies of the planning apparatus and the cumbersome bureaucracy
- the intervention of the state, which meant that business had to work within a framework set by the regime
- the competing demands of the different branches of the armed forces.

So Germany would enter the Second World War in what was essentially quite an uneconomic fashion because attempts to fully mobilise the economy took place during the war itself.

The wartime economy and Speer

The expansion of the rearmament programme between 1936 and 1939 and the move towards total war after 1942 have been the subject of rigorous debate among historians. Some have argued that rearmament in the period after 1936 was an improvised measure and part of a programme to reduce unemployment. It was never intended as preparation for either a short-term or a major world war. These historians

Synthetic products Manufacturing substitutes that were needed to prevent Germany having to rely on foreign imports of the raw materials required for industrial and military expansion.

Guns not butter This was the 'choice' Göring proposed between consumer products and weapons. In December 1936 he is quoted as saying: 'I tell you guns make us powerful. Butter only makes us fat.'

Exam tip

Consider the view that German militarisation had been mismanaged in the period 1933–39.

Total war A phrase used to describe the Nazi aim to harness all their resources into the war effort.

further argue that war preparation was an insignificant part of the economy in the period 1933–39. The figure for 1938, for example, only represented 15% of the gross national expenditure. The mobilisation of the whole of the German economy for war would have placed enormous strains on the economy and Hitler was afraid that this could lead to civilian unrest. He could not be sure that German people would endure prolonged social and economic sacrifices.

However, others have argued for a direct link between the Four-Year Plan and the outbreak of the Second World War because government military expenditure significantly increased between 1933 and 1939, as indicated in Table 8. Why rearm, they argue, unless it was because of a desire for war, and how were Nazi foreign policy aims and objectives to be achieved without rearmament?

Table 8 Military expenditure between 1933 and 1939

Year	Military expenditure
1933	1.9 billion marks
1936	5.8 billion marks
1938	18.4 billion marks
1939	32.3 billion marks

Whichever version you subscribe to there is no altering the fact that an expanded rearmament programme created a vicious circle as seen in Figure 1:

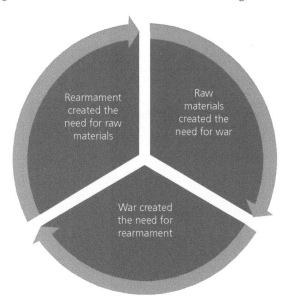

Figure 1 Rearmament: the vicious circle

This in itself has opened up another debate on economic policy in relation to whether the economy had been made hostage to war preparation because of an ideological drive, or whether it was a response to an economic crisis inside Germany brought on by domestic factors. Regardless of your view, the rearmament programme that began in 1933 was ultimately to be paid for by exploiting the resources of other captured economies. Germany was unable to secure self-sufficiency in raw materials by 1939, and so would have to rely upon a plunder economy.

The wars of expansion therefore almost by default became the main driver of the Nazi economy. The ultimate goal was a self-sufficient war economy sustained through territorial expansion. Rearmament would provide the means for achieving Lebensraum. Policies of autarky and Lebensraum taken together reveal the distinctly nationalist nature of Nazi economic policy.

Autarky Economic self sufficiency.

However, the German economy turned out to be far less adaptable to total war than the regime could have imagined. Germany's economic potential had been squandered early in the war through the inefficient management of resources. Indeed, there were a number of serious shortcomings.

- There was no central agency and no coherent plan. The economics ministry, the finance ministry, the office of the Four-Year Plan and the armed forces all went their own ways.
- There was no coherent plan for the allocation of resources. This led to shortages in some areas and duplication in others. The army, for example, imposed its own priorities in the production of munitions.
- The three branches of the armed services refused to integrate their production requirements, and this led to conflicting priorities, rivalries and in-fighting. The result was expensive and slow-moving production programmes.
- Relations between the civilian and military authorities were strained. The transfer of authority to Göring's largely civilian administration created tensions.
- Layer upon layer of economic bureaucracy stifled initiatives from industry and science and created a slow and cumbersome apparatus of control for what was supposed to be a managed economy based on state intervention. The command economy was unable to effectively command.
- Technical refinements and excessively high standards of workmanship reduced production.
- By 1942, Germany was failing to produce weapons in sufficient quantities to ensure military victory.

Enter Albert Speer.

He came to prominence in spring 1942 when Hitler nominated him as minister for armaments. By 1944 he had assumed responsibility for the entire German war economy and he effectively provided Hitler with his fight to the finish.

Speer saw the war effort purely in terms of logistics, and brought with him a more corporate solution to the mobilisation of resources. He wanted to harness all available effort into the total war. This meant diverting all workers from non-essential industries into war production. In April 1942, he created the Central Planning Board, which allocated raw materials to the most essential sectors. He arranged for the redistribution of the workforce, the increase in the female labour force and the recruitment or conscription of foreign workers.

By 1944, weapons production had trebled. Speer was successful in maintaining high levels of war production, but his success was tempered by a number of considerable problems.

- He was never able to plan a fully consistent policy because of certain internal obstacles, and because resources were being rapidly eaten up by the demands of a prolonged war that Germany was losing.

- His non-ideological approach attracted enemies. Ideological objectors resisted Speer's attempts to employ women and to improve the camp conditions of the foreign labour force. Speer was concerned about the wastage of the potential of the foreign workforce.
- There was a continuous shortage of raw materials and lack of labour. Time and manpower were wasted in moving factories underground, and men, weapons and radar were redirected to protect German cities from Allied bombing.
- Military defeat and incessant allied bombing handicapped the effectiveness of Speer's central office. Allied bombing decreased Germany's armaments production by 50%.
- Speer was undermined by divisions in responsibility. Fritz Sauckel was minister for labour and Himmler was in charge of the concentration camps. There was a breakdown in communications because Nazi Germany continued to be top heavy with officialdom and bureaucracy.

Summary

When you have completed this section, you should have a thorough knowledge of the effectiveness of Nazi economic policies in the period 1933–45.

- Schacht established a delicate balance between consumer confidence and military needs through investment, regulation and incentives.
- The Nazi regime created a command economy by extending government controls over the economy with the help of Schacht, Göring and Speer.
- Göring created a conflict over economic priorities through initiatives such as 'guns or butter'.
- There were changes in economic priorities during the period.
- Speer rationalised industry and increased the workforce by recruiting women and foreign workers.
- There was a contrasting impact of Nazi economic policies on different groups such as women, the workers and big business.

Changes in foreign policy and the Second World War

What were the key drivers for German foreign policy?

The factors that shaped the agenda, contours and execution of German foreign policy in the period after 1933 have been the subject of continuous historical debate. These discussions tend to attribute different degrees of importance to a variety of key drivers, which include:

- domestic policy
- historical tradition
- economic priorities
- the international landscape
- leadership.

Exam tip

When reaching an overall judgement about the effectiveness of Nazi economic policies you should consider the different priorities of the regime at different times.

Domestic policy

To what extent was Nazi domestic policy designed to help Hitler achieve his foreign policy objectives, or was it a propaganda device to mobilise support for the regime?

The case for design

Conditions at home may affect the way in which foreign policy is conducted. Nazi domestic policy had been based on a specific ideological programme that stemmed from a mutated form of nationalism. The ideology of racial supremacy was extended through the principle of Social Darwinism. The creation of a Volksgemeinschaft and the purification of the race were seen by some historians as the preliminary steps in the Nazi pursuit of an expansionist foreign policy and the creation of a new European or even global order.

The case for propaganda

However, other historians have challenged the view that Nazi philosophy eventually shaped the nature and extent of German foreign policy. They argue that Nazi foreign policy was nothing more than a tool of propaganda. It existed in a world of slogans rather than concrete aims — a series of vague and undefined notions that allowed the German people to indulge in an ultimately unrealistic vision of territorial conquest.

Historical tradition

To what extent can Nazi foreign policy represent either continuity with the main themes of German history or a break with the past?

The case for continuity

It has been argued that Hitler's foreign policy was essentially a playing out of the past. It perpetuated ideas and behaviours evident in German history from Bismarck onwards, and was rooted in traditional German power policy. Indeed, national self-assertion through expansion of German power was a continuous thread running throughout German foreign policy There was therefore a consistency to a foreign policy aimed at conflict and expansionism and based on feelings of insecurity, dissatisfaction or resentment.

Some elements of Hitler's foreign policy could be seen as a continuation of policies established by Gustav Stresemann in the 1920s. Stresemann operated a policy of revisionism: he wanted changes to the terms of the Treaty of Versailles as they affected Germany. Above all, he wanted to release Germany from the crippling burden of the reparations payments demanded in the treaty. Although Stresemann's methods were peaceful and diplomatic — he signed the Locarno Treaties, which pledged that Germany wouldn't go to war, and he was awarded the Nobel Peace Prize in 1926 — it is also the case that he probably didn't rule out the possibility of the use of force to regain territories lost to Poland at Versailles.

It is possible to conclude that Stresemann's peaceful approach was partly pragmatic, as the Weimar Republic was in no fit state to enter any conflict. We could argue that a policy of revisionism would have led to adjustments to the international order regardless of who was in power in Germany. German leaders of any stripe were always going to challenge what they saw as the unfinished business of the First World War: therefore Hitler's brand of revisionism, though far more aggressive than Stresemann's, was not a new departure.

Social Darwinism
The principle of the survival of the fittest, which could best be expressed in expansionist wars.

Exam tip

Beware of the idea that Nazi foreign policy merely grew out of propaganda. This view is essentially flawed because it ignores the precise historical context of foreign policy developments and relies on the premise that the German people were capable of being completely seduced by propaganda.

Otto von Bismarck
Chancellor of the German empire between 1871 and 1890. He wanted to improve Germany's diplomatic position in Europe.

Revisionism The policy of attempting to revise the terms of the 1919 Treaty of Versailles as they affected Germany.

Knowledge check 17

Was there a continuous thread in German foreign policy in the period 1890–1933?

The case for change

To see Hitler as a pure revisionist until 1938 and an expansionist afterwards does not hold water for some historians. Hitler had a corrupted vision of foreign policy that was dominated by visions of race and space (Lebensraum), which distinguished it from earlier periods. He saw revisionism as merely a prelude, with the overture coming later in the form of continental and possibly global domination.

Economic priorities

To what extent was Hitler a prisoner of capitalist forces inside Germany that were seeking to profit from territorial expansion?

The case for big business and expansion

It has been argued that foreign policy was driven by economic considerations in the period after 1933. By this view, Hitler was merely a pawn in the hands of German capitalists who saw the profitability of accelerating the pace of rearmament and investment in expansionist wars abroad.

It has also been argued that an aggressive foreign policy was a way of releasing internal social and economic discontent by converting it into support for the regime through foreign adventures. In other words, it was a way of preserving domestic order through social imperialism.

The case against big business and expansion

The link between big business and aggressive Nazi foreign policy has been challenged on the grounds that business would have profited more from a revival in economic links rather than through wars of aggression, which always carried the risk of failure. This was especially the case in relation to the Soviet Union.

Hitler did not need capitalists to tell him that the east could provide him with essential raw materials which could benefit German industry, such as iron ore, manganese, coal, nickel, molybdenum and oil. He sought the productive soil of eastern Europe to support the Aryan state. Hitler's economic organisation and his pre-war diplomacy were part of the same drive towards wars of expansion and acquisition.

The international landscape

To what extent did Hitler merely react to international developments, or weigh up the advantages of shaping them?

The case for reactive

A foreign policy should adapt to the needs or opportunities that present themselves within the international environment. International security, as it was established in the 1920s, was anything but secure. The fragile safeguards that the League of Nations had implemented to secure a lasting peace were increasingly undermined by a series of challenges to its authority. In 1931, Japan seized Manchuria, an important economic region in north-east China. Italy invaded Abyssinia in 1935.

Exam tip

Foreign policy can be influenced by a range of different interest groups. Look carefully at the aims of Gustav Stresemann in 1925 and the army leaders in 1926.

Social imperialism A defensive political strategy that channels internal criticism of domestic policy into support for foreign wars of expansion.

Exam tip

A word of caution: the view that Hitler was a puppet in the capitalists' hands is an extreme Marxist interpretation of foreign policy, unashamedly offering an economic explanation for wars of aggression and territorial expansion.

League of Nations This body established the principle of collective security among nations in the aftermath of the First World War.

The league's failure to stand up to acts of international aggression persuaded Hitler that he could take risks. Hitler saw international relations as a jungle in which the only guiding star was unilateral self-interest. Within this jungle he could test the stress points and at the same time be prepared to form tactical alliances in order to secure his objectives.

The case for proactive

Germany's concentration on national interests was inevitably going to lead to a realignment with the country's continental neighbours. If Germany was to recover its status as a great power, then the task went beyond mere diplomacy. Hitler had no interest in maintaining mechanisms that would establish European stability, and he did not feel obliged to adhere to the rules of multi-lateral diplomacy and protocol that had been established through what he saw as an artificial process of collective decision making. His clear goal was the removal of obstacles in the path of German power.

Leadership

Historians are divided over the extent to which Nazi foreign policy was mainly driven by Hitler. Some claim that it originated from Hitler's long-term plan to create a racially pure Germanic empire through eastwards expansion.

Others argue that it had nothing to do with Hitler's personal determination to achieve a long-term goal of expansion, but was a pragmatic response to the changing domestic and international arena.

The case for race and space

Hitler introduced a definite change of policy after 1933 to rearm, to remove the burdens of Versailles, and to establish a new order of racial purity through eastwards expansion. Hitler had a grand design based upon a plan in stages, or Stufenplan as seen in Figure 2.

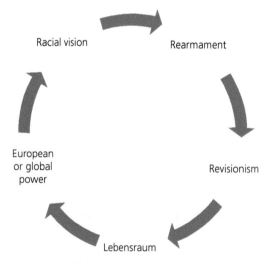

Racial vision

Rearmament

Revisionism

Lebensraum

European or global power

Figure 2 The pursuit of race and space

> ### Knowledge check 18
>
> Find examples of tactical agreements signed by the German government in the period 1934–39.

Some have argued that if contemporary politicians had taken *Mein Kampf* more seriously, they would have recognised Hitler's territorial ambitions well in advance and could then have adopted a more rigorous response. The German achievements in foreign policy by 1938 bore a remarkable resemblance to those outlined in the Hossbach Memorandum and elsewhere.

The economy was being mobilised for war. Economic development, the racial vision and territorial expansion went hand in hand. Hitler wanted to establish an empire based on race. The pursuit of Lebensraum had some concrete meaning, even if its path was not completely charted.

The case for expansion without object

There is a difference between strategic aims and visionary orientations.

It has been claimed that in foreign policy, Hitler was nothing more than a poseur with confused aims and objectives that were only on occasion turned into hard facts and concrete truths. As a result, it is unclear what his precise intentions were. It is perhaps easier to consider that territorial expansion eastwards was one of a range of possibilities.

Rather than accepting the view that Hitler had a long-term plan for European or global conquest, it could be argued that his aggressive foreign policy after 1937 should be attributed to a deepening economic crisis in Germany brought on by overspending on rearmament.

Furthermore, it could be argued that it was the changing economic and political climate of the 1930s — the impact of the Depression, and the diplomatic isolation of America and the Soviet Union — that created the conditions for expansion and war, not Hitler. He merely took advantage of them.

Conclusion

Ideology, economic priorities, the changing international landscape, a national tradition and national ambition all played their part in determining the nature and extent of Nazi foreign policy between 1933 and 1939, but the decisive factor appears to be leadership.

The aims and objectives of Nazi foreign policy up to 1939

Not all foreign policy can be spelled out in a clear and defined way. In fact, the aims and objectives of foreign policy are often broad and slightly vague, as policy can change at any given moment in time, in relation not only to the national interest and the international arena, but also the changing political leadership of the home nation.

If we accept that Hitler's foreign policy was a logical extension of earlier foreign policy, then clearly Hitler and his generals did not believe that the frontiers of 1914 or indeed 1918 were sufficient. Germany was already pursuing an expansionist path well before Hitler adopted and adapted it into a programme for Lebensraum combined with a racist ideology. The revisionism of Weimar was only the starting point for Hitler and would be replaced in time by not only Machiavellian expediency but also a degree of additional planning.

Knowledge check 19

What was the Hossbach Memorandum?

There are three major sources for uncovering Hitler's aims and objectives for foreign policy:

1 *Mein Kampf*, 'My struggle', dictated by Hitler in Landsberg prison following the Munich Putsch of 1923.

2 *Zweites Buch*, or the 'Second book', which dealt with foreign policy exclusively but was unpublished in Hitler's lifetime.

3 *Tischgespräche*, or 'Table talk', a series of spoken remarks edited by Dr Henry Picker, a member of Hitler's executive staff.

Exam tip

These works are undisciplined and rambling in nature and so it is difficult to arrive at a carefully structured outline on policy.

Of course, Hitler would take advantage of any uncertainty and hesitation within the international community to secure what have been identified as three specific areas of policy. Although it is claimed that he did not have a clearly predetermined timetable, his objectives seem consistent, and involved:

- the full revision of the Treaty of Versailles in Germany's interest
- the inclusion of all people of German race within an enlarged Reich
- the increase of living space for Germany's large population in the east through the conquest of Lebensraum.

Historians have differed over how far Hitler's pursuit of these objectives was planned in advance, and how much came down to taking advantage of international circumstances in the period 1933–39. Table 9 looks at how successive actions can be regarded.

Table 9 Planning versus opportunism in Hitler's European actions

Year and event	Part of a planned programme of territorial expansion in stages?	An opportunist response to the changing international arena?
1932–33 Geneva Disarmament Conference	Hitler withdrew from the disarmament talks because any arms control scheme, however generous to Germany, would reduce the country's capacity to rearm. Hitler wanted to revive Germany's military power. By 1934 he had increased the army to 240,000 men. In March 1935, the existence of the German air force was admitted. A week later military conscription was introduced.	Hitler took advantage of differences between France and Britain over German parity at the disarmament talks.
October 1933 Germany withdrew from the League of Nations	Hitler disagreed in principle with multinational bodies such as the League of Nations, which he believed only perpetuated Germany's second-class status. He found multinational negotiations tedious and Germany's withdrawal was always very likely given the commitment to rearmament.	He exploited a favourable diplomatic climate that stemmed from the growing fear of Communist Russia. A powerful German state in the centre of Europe was seen as a useful bulwark against the spread of communism. The Depression turned the attention of governments inwards towards their own domestic problems.
1936 The Rhineland was remilitarised	The recovery of full sovereignty in the Rhineland was a major policy objective. Remilitarisation was an essential prelude to any revision of Germany's eastern boundaries. By shoring up the gap on its western frontier, Germany could block a French offensive in aid of Poland.	Italy's invasion of Abyssinia had distracted Britain and France. Hitler took advantage of this in his move to remilitarise the Rhineland. France was occupied by a general election that exposed deep divisions in the country. The election brought a socialist/Communist alliance to power. Hitler took the opportunity to consolidate his power in Germany.

Year and event	Part of a planned programme of territorial expansion in stages?	An opportunist response to the changing international arena?
1938 Anschluss with Austria	Since the collapse of the Austro-Hungarian empire at the end of the First World War, German nationalists had harboured a desire for a union between Austria and Germany. It was part of Hitler's dream of a greater Germany and the German domination of central Europe. Anschluss could also provide many economic advantages, such as access to the Austrian gold reserves and mineral deposits of copper and lead.	Mussolini had turned his attention away from supporting Austrian independence towards acquiring an overseas empire. Austria could no longer rely on Italian support. The Schuschnigg plebiscite triggered Anschluss. The Japanese invasion of Manchuria revealed the advantage of an aggressive foreign policy, because the aggressor had been allowed to triumph. Britain was committed to appeasement of German demands and France was still distracted by political divisions. This allowed Hitler to pursue his interests in Austria.
1938 Czech crisis	There were 3.5 million German people living in the Sudetenland in western Czechoslovakia, which Hitler wanted to incorporate within the Third Reich. They were seen in Germany as a disadvantaged minority. The neutralisation of Czechoslovakia was high on the list of any revisionist programme. For Hitler, an independent Czechoslovakia was a barrier to German control of central Europe. Czechoslovakia also had a strong army and alliances with both France and Russia. It was also a source of raw materials for Hitler's rearmament programme.	Hitler exploited grievances among ethnic German people about the predominance of Czech officials in German-speaking areas. He exploited Konrad Henlein's Sudeten German Party to make impossible demands on the Czech government. Hitler took advantage of the British policy of appeasement.
1939 The occupation of Bohemia and Moravia	The annexation of the rump of Czechoslovakia followed, despite the four-power guarantee that had been established at the Munich Conference of 29 September 1938. There were serious differences between the provinces of Bohemia and Slovakia. Hitler exploited the ethnic diversity of the country as a lever to break up Czechoslovakia. This illustrated that Hitler had clear plans beyond revisions of the Treaty of Versailles, and the uniting of German-speaking peoples. This was part of an imperialist expansion that threatened the non-Germans of Eastern Europe.	Hitler used as a pretext the claim that there was mistreatment of the remaining German minority in Czechoslovakia. This was another calculated probe to test the willingness of the Allies to resort to force.
1939 Poland	The Non-Aggression Pact with Poland in 1934 was really a 'no aggression yet' pact, because Hitler had a long-term plan to absorb the remaining German population of Poland into Germany. It had always been part of the revisionist programme to take back Posen and West Prussia, which had been removed from Germany at Versailles. The loss of these territories had led to the division of Germany, with East Prussia isolated by the creation of the Polish Corridor. At the Hossbach Conference of November 1937 it was made a priority to take these territories back. Hitler stated his aims for eastward expansion and Lebensraum.	Hitler used once again the pretext of mistreatment of the German minority in Poland in September 1939. He gambled that Britain and France would back down because they were incapable of honouring their guarantees to Poland.

Year and event	Part of a planned programme of territorial expansion in stages?	An opportunist response to the changing international arena?
	In August 1939, Germany signed a Non-Aggression Pact with Russia, which made it harder for the West to protect Poland. The occupation of Poland would provide a launchpad for a later attack on Russia.	
	The Gleiwitz Radio Station incident, a fabricated attack on a German radio station, was used along with a number of other incidents as examples of Polish aggression towards Germany, justifying the German invasion. But the actions were all planned and staged by the SS.	

Schuschnigg plebiscite In February 1938 the Austrian chancellor, Schuschnigg, was bullied into granting the Austrian Nazi Party freedom of activity and accepting a Nazi nominee into his cabinet. On returning to Austria he instead ordered a plebiscite on maintaining Austrian independence, which would have been accepted, it is estimated, by 70% of Austrians. Hitler ordered that the plebiscite be cancelled and forced Schuschnigg to resign.

Hitler clearly had long-term aims and objectives, but he was also prepared to take advantage of any opportunities that came along to further his plans.

The factors that favoured German expansion after 1936

- The Axis agreement with Italy created an arrangement for mutual self-interest. This allowed Germany free reign in Austria.
- The Anti-Comintern Pact broadened the Axis agreement to include Japan. In so doing it fixed the fronts for the Second World War.
- The paralysis of the League of Nations provided Germany with an opportunity to build up a network of bilateral agreements that effectively undermined the principle of collective security.
- France was effectively isolated. Germany was able to construct agreements with France's potential ally Russia.
- The Soviet Union was effectively isolated because of the belief that Soviet communism was the real danger to European stability and not Germany. Soviet involvement in the Spanish Civil War intensified British and French suspicions. The Western powers were consequently unable to secure a pact with Russia in 1939, which would have made the guarantees they gave to Poland a practical military proposition. In the event, the West was incapable of saving Poland.
- Appeasement merely sharpened the spur of injustice Germany felt. It reinforced Hitler's belief that the German state had been compressed and repressed following the First World War. By accepting some of Hitler's arguments, the appeasers in effect precipitated war.

Appeasement Neville Chamberlain, the British prime minister, was among those who believed that Hitler could be restrained if concessions were given to some of his demands. This ultimately built up Nazi self-confidence.

Gleiwitz Radio Station incident A piece of Nazi propaganda which alleged that the Poles had opened hostilities by attempting to seize the radio station in Silesia.

Knowledge check 20

What was the significance of the Munich Conference of 29 September 1938?

The Second World War

Active and passive forces at work

The active forces

German expansionism was the principal cause of war.

Hitler had been catapulted into power on a programme of national revival and self-assertion. This was always likely to be reflected in his foreign policy and handling of international relations. The shift in economic priorities from a defensive rearmament programme to the preparation of highly militarised and mechanised forces did not bode well.

If Germany was going to establish a continental empire, colonies in Africa and the destruction of the Soviet Union, this was not going to happen through negotiation. Germany would not be subdued by regional security pacts, arms limitation agreements or the League of Nations. Hitler's foreign policy programme could only be achieved through war, as the Nuremberg Judgement confirmed.

The passive forces

Nazi foreign policy should be placed in the context of international relations in the 1930s. You need to measure the extent to which Hitler was able to influence the course of world affairs due to international circumstances.

The legacy of the First World War and the Versailles settlement had sowed the seeds for international disputes in the future. The fact that there were disputed borders and German irredenta in eastern Europe created the potential for instability despite the Locarno spirit of the 1920s.

There were also a number of passive forces at work.

- The Depression exploded the myth of international stability. It led to social and economic problems everywhere, but in Germany it fed the aggressive programme of National Socialism. In the West, it delayed the potential for rearmament and created an atmosphere of mutual suspicion and recrimination. The Depression, therefore, placed a barrier in the way of effective collaboration against the growth of aggressive nationalism.
- The Treaty of Versailles of 1919 had poisoned international relations throughout the 1920s and 30s. The treaty in itself was strong enough to contain a resurgent Germany, but the failure to collectively enforce its terms provided Hitler with opportunities to pursue German objectives.
- The League of Nations was ineffective as a preserver of peace. As far as Hitler was concerned, he saw the league as a club of victorious powers that was forcing an unjust peace upon Germany. The association of the league with the Treaty of Versailles meant that there was an inherent barrier to its acceptance as an impartial peacemaker.
- Britain and France had held a flawed belief that Hitler was a reasonable politician who would accept the compromises within international settlements. As a result, they were prepared to make repeated concessions to Hitler until they finally stood firm over Poland.

Nuremberg Judgement The military tribunals held at Nuremberg after the war blamed Hitler and his policy for the outbreak of the Second World War.

Irredenta German minorities under the control of other countries such as Czechoslovakia.

Exam tip

The Nuremberg Judgement has been challenged by some historians. It has been argued that Hitler was merely pursuing traditional foreign policy aims and that he did not follow either a specific plan or long-term objectives for war.

Knowledge check 21

What was the Locarno spirit?

The actions of Western leaders unintentionally accelerated Hitler's progress towards war, but they did not cause it. Moreover, to have acted sooner against Hitler would probably have precipitated the earlier outbreak of war.

German successes in Western Europe

Despite the misjudged assurances from Ribbentrop to Hitler that Britain and France would not go to war over the occupation of Poland, both countries declared war when Germany did not agree to withdraw its troops. Hitler had no option but to extend the war to other fronts.

In April 1940, Denmark and Norway became the first casualties of Blitzkrieg, which allowed the German navy to gain strategic access to the North Atlantic. They were followed by the Low Countries. Even before the Polish campaign was over, plans were set in motion for the German invasion of Belgium, Holland and Luxembourg.

The German Panzers bypassed the Maginot Line and the French defences on the Belgian frontier with a rapid advance through the Ardennes Forest in June 1940. France fell on 19 June 1940.

The British Expeditionary Force was pushed back to the beaches of Dunkirk by late May 1940 and mainland Europe became fortress Germany. The speed and scale of the victories reinforced Hitler's belief in June 1940 that the war in the west had come to an end, and that Britain would come to the negotiating table and accept a compromised peace.

The conflict that originally focused on western Europe eventually took on global characteristics when the Germans invaded the Soviet Union.

The invasion of the Soviet Union

The quest for Lebensraum

Following the failure of the West to involve the Soviet Union in a common front that they hoped would deter Hitler, the Molotov–Ribbentrop Pact was signed on 23 August 1939.

On the one hand this represented a major ideological and diplomatic turnaround for the Nazis, given Hitler's open hostility towards communism. However, it should also be noted that despite the ideological divide, there had always been commercial contracts between the two nations.

The treaties of Rapallo in 1922 and Berlin in 1926 had established a mutually advantageous relationship and ironically it was probably Russian economic assistance which prevented the early collapse of the German war machine, because it helped to neutralise the British blockade. The Russians provided raw materials directly to Germany or allowed them to be transported across Russian territories.

The published text of the Non-Aggression Pact had prevented both powers from supporting any country at war with either of the signatories. However, the secret clauses referred to as the 'boundaries of the mutual spheres of influence' in eastern Europe, were tantamount to a booty pact because they divided Poland between Germany and the Soviet Union as well as allocating other regional territories to each other.

Joachim von Ribbentrop Ribbentrop was Germany's foreign minister, appointed in 1938. He was nicknamed Ribbensnob and Brickendrop by his contemporaries on account of his pomposity and lack of intellect.

Blitzkrieg A strategy for rapid deployment of mechanised warfare using troops, tanks and air power.

Maginot Line A line of French defences and fortifications built along France's borders with Italy, Switzerland and Germany, but not extending all the way north to the English Channel.

Blockade An attempt to prevent goods and materials from entering or leaving a country.

Despite the Non-Aggression Pact, Hitler had always intended to invade the Soviet Union. Now that Germany and the Soviet Union shared a common frontier in Poland, it would be easier for Germany to exploit this advantage when the time was right.

The negative outcome for Germany of the Battle of Britain and the fact that Operation Sealion had to be abandoned merely strengthened Hitler's resolve to attack the Soviet Union. By November 1940 military preparations for Operation Barbarossa were in place. The invasion of Russia, which was supposed to be another Blitzkrieg war, began on 22 June 1941.

The invasion of the Soviet Union was at the core of a racist version of Social Darwinism. This distinguished Nazi foreign policy from anything which had come before. Hitler viewed Russia as an ideological enemy, a monstrous regime led by racially unfit Jewish people. The Nazis also considered Slavic people to be racially inferior.

The war against Russia was not only a crusade against Bolshevism, it was a war for plunder for the large reservoir of Slav labour, the oil reserves of the Caucasus and the grain supplies of Ukraine. The focus of everything in the east that Hitler had written about in *Mein Kampf* became a reality. This was also a pre-emptive strike against an enemy that had as yet unrealised military potential. The Soviet Union had the ability, if fully mobilised, to pose a strategic threat to Germany's European empire.

The timing of the invasion was based upon the misleading premise that the Soviet Union had limited resources and a limited military capacity at its disposal. There were initial apparent successes, which included the siege of Leningrad, and the taking of three million Soviet prisoners during the course of the invasion.

However, early promises of success were not fulfilled because the Germans overextended their lines of communication and suffered from inadequate reserves. The German army was unprepared for a long Soviet campaign. Its defeat at Stalingrad became one of the major turning points of the war.

The Wannsee Conference and the Final Solution

From resettlement to annihilation

The infamous meeting at the lakeside villa near Berlin in January 1942 grew out of a directive to draft a programme for a 'final solution' to the 'Jewish problem'. Heydrich had ominously referred to his resettlement programme as the territorial final solution. This alone did not augur well for Jewish people.

As resettlement became a logistical nightmare because of the scale of the operation, the Nazis resolved upon organised mass murder as the preferred solution. In fact, Hitler had predicted as much in a speech in the Reichstag on 30 January 1939. The Wannsee Conference finalised the administration of mass murder.

However, the twisted path to Auschwitz has itself been the subject of rigorous debate. Some see the organised mass murder of Jewish people as part of long-planned phases of anti-Semitic policy, which were put into effect separately according to the particular need. It amounted to the planned destruction of a race in stages.

Operation Sealion (In German, Unternehmen Seelöwe): The codename for the plan for the invasion of Britain.

Defeat at Stalingrad The long and bloody Battle of Stalingrad (23 August 1942– 2 February 1943) ended with a Soviet victory. The German army was surrounded and had to surrender.

Auschwitz Part of the network of Nazi extermination camps where millions were murdered.

Others see it as a process of cumulative radicalism brought on by the experience of war, a response to initiatives introduced by different authorities within the Nazi organisation or just pathological improvisation.

The reality, however, is that the T4 action had been a precursor to the death camps. The euthanasia programme to kill people with mental disabilities meant that organised mass murder had already been tried and tested. The T4 personnel were transferred to the east to supervise the next major instalment of mass murder. These people had already shown that they held no moral scruples about the killings they undertook in the name of the Reich.

As a result, the Wannsee Conference only gave a retrospective sanction to a policy that had already been decided and adopted.

The factors leading to the defeat of Germany by 1945

Leadership, military strategy and outcomes, and resources

Wars are complex processes which are not just decided by fulcrum moments on the battlefield. The outcomes of battles are often uncertain even when long-term military preparations and logistics have been meticulously planned. Aggressive nationalism may have been a trigger for the Nazis to unleash war on Europe, but this was not enough to ensure success, even if it was supported by an unhealthy measure of self-confidence.

Leadership

Hitler convinced the generals of the achievability of certain territorial goals even though Germany did not have the necessary economic resources. This was a high-risk strategy for expansion, especially when he did not consider that military preparedness was a relative concept when gauged against the potential of your enemy.

Hitler had not made allowances for either the resilience of the opposition or its capacity for endurance. He was also unwilling to sanction organised military retreat or consider that discretion was sometimes the better part of valour in conflicts. His belief in his own infallibility and in the willpower and determination of the German people meant that he was prepared to destroy the structure of the high command in Germany, which was a well-oiled machine of military command. He was clearly not prepared to accept the advice of those with the acumen and experience to provide it.

The German declaration of war on the USA seems the petulant reaction of a leader who had lost touch with reality. Hitler had no appreciation of the enormous strategic implications of the entry of the USA into the war, and miscalculated that it would become bogged down with conflicts in the Pacific.

Military strategy and outcomes

The ease of the early victories in the west boosted Hitler's self-confidence and his prestige in Germany. He became delusional about the powers of his own superior strategic thinking.

Exam tip

The economic potential of a country for war is inextricably interwoven with the quality of effective leadership and performance in the theatres of warfare. They are all interdependent on each other and any open-ended essay response should reflect this.

- He misread the British position, which would not accept enforced changes to the international order or potential threats to the British empire. His 'peace offer' in a speech to the Reichstag on 19 July 1940 was flatly rejected.
- Operation Sealion lacked any sense of total commitment and relied on the premise of German air superiority, which was not achieved.
- The negative outcome of the Battle of Britain merely strengthened his resolve to attack Russia.
- The extension of the war in north Africa and the inclusion of the USA were a direct consequence of his inability to defeat Russia.
- The surrender of 300,000 German troops in Stalingrad marked the beginning of the Russian counter-offensive.
- Global warfare became a desperate attempt to escalate the war because of the impasse that Hitler had driven himself into.
- By the end of 1941 Hitler had reached the zenith of his power in Europe.

Hitler's decision to switch to attacking Russia before defeating Britain and then his declaration of war on the USA before defeating Russia revealed a flawed tactical approach to warfare. By leaving an undefeated Britain in the west, and an undefeated Soviet Union in the east, both backed by a hugely powerful USA, he had repeated a very serious strategic error. He had also created a war on two fronts which, ironically, his early diplomacy had striven hard to avoid.

Resources

Hitler ignored warnings that Germany's economy had not developed sufficiently to wage a global conflict. Subsequent events exposed that he was driven by an ideological mentality that was unable to accept economic and military truths. His preference for offensive rather than defensive weapons led to massive over-investment in the V1 and V2 rocket programmes.

V1 and V2 rockets Unmanned German rockets that were used to terrorise the civilian population of Britain.

There was a fundamental underestimation of Soviet economic potential, national resources and bureaucratic organisation. In the Soviet Union, German lines became overextended and the supply of ammunition, food, petrol, spares and battle dress failed to keep up with demand. The thrust into Ukraine and the Caucasus exposed that this was a war for which Germany was ill-prepared and lacked the capacity to sustain. When the rains came, the mechanised German forces struggled in the mud of the undeveloped Soviet road network.

The American Lend-Lease Act of 1941 meant that Britain and later Russia could be supplied with all the military equipment they needed until the end of the war. When the USA entered the war later that year, the writing was really on the wall. America's greater industrial capacity exposed Germany's weakness. Allied bombing raids seriously damaged Germany's industry, with production of armaments cut by 50%, and damaged transport and communications networks.

Lend-Lease Act This was agreed by the American Congress in March 1941. It permitted President Roosevelt to sell or lend any type of war material to any country whose defence seemed vital to the interests of the United States.

The impact of the war on different sections of German society

The Second World War was a total war. This meant that the entire populations of the belligerent nations were involved. The burden of warfare therefore fell just as heavily on the civilian population.

The German people became subject to arbitrary and unlimited state power. The war resulted in the government of the Reich being even more of a battlefield of competing factions, especially when Hitler made fewer public appearances towards the end of the war.

The Second World War cast a shadow over the civilian population of Germany, but the impact was uneven and disproportionate in terms of suffering and loss. The war affected German society in different ways and also affected the relationship between individuals and the state.

The impact on social order

The war led to further terrorisation of the civilian population. On the one hand, through his propaganda Joseph Goebbels fed the people a carefully blended mix of hope, fear, threats and promises in order to maintain their confidence in Hitler's leadership. He emphasised the consequences of Germany's defeat at the hands of the barbaric Soviet Union. On the other hand, draconian measures were employed to deter civilians from adopting a defeatist attitude. This resulted in increased levels of police vigilance and harsher wartime penalties, which were often totally disproportionate to the alleged offences. For example, in Brandenburg penitentiary alone, there were 2,042 executions between 1940 and 1945.

The impact on social unity

Allied bombing raids such as the thousand-bomber raids on Cologne and Hamburg deliberately pinpointed civilian morale, which they now saw as a legitimate target. However, in Germany just as in Britain, carpet bombing of cities often had the opposite effect. It revealed the capacity of the German people to remain stoical. The League of German Maidens and the Hitler Youth were praised for rallying to support those who lost their homes and the injured.

Total war meant that young people were needed to help with the harvests, and the age of conscription was reduced to 17 in 1943 and 16 by 1945. In a desperate attempt to raise more troops, boys as young as 11 were drafted from the Hitler Youth into the Volkssturm and fought in the front line.

There were signs of conflict, tension and opposition among sections of younger people. There were some acts of defiance such as the distribution of anti-Nazi leaflets by student groups such as the White Rose, led by Hans and Sophie Scholl, and by youth groups such as the Edelweiss Pirates. There were relatively small numbers of such activists. However, the fact that there were 3,393 executions in 1942, 5,684 in 1943 and 5,764 in 1944 gives a sense of the growing dissatisfaction of many people with the Third Reich.

On the whole, however, public confidence in Hitler's regime remained high and the majority of people stayed loyal to Hitler to the bitter end.

Following the defeat of Germany in 1945, the Allied occupation forces pursued a policy of denazification of German society. This was an attempt to break the Nazi ideological bond that had held German society together and to sweep away the Volksgemeinschaft which Hitler had shaped. The Allies embarked on a crusade of converting the German people from Nazism to democracy.

Volkssturm This was effectively a home guard made up of young people, people with disabilities and older people. They faced not only aerial bombing, but machine guns, artillery and tanks.

The impact on the social fabric of society

The social fabric of German society was driven by tensions between refugees and the indigenous population, especially in the rural areas, which were traditionally more conservative in outlook.

As the war progressed, there was an influx of millions of refugees, most of whom had fled before the advancing Soviet armies. By 1944, there was also a foreign workforce of some 8 million people in Germany. General ignorance of these dislocated people led to misunderstandings, fear and discrimination on the part of the resident population.

Shortened war rations and the worsening of labour and housing conditions led to a slow erosion of the hopes and aspirations of the German people. Shortages, the black market and bombing raids disrupted the normal workings of society, and the stepping up of the war economy meant that many people had to change their jobs to work in war production. Overwork and exhaustion ate into the lives of the civilian population and morale inevitably suffered.

The demands of total war meant the Nazis were forced to modify their policy towards women, reversing the ideological prerogatives that they had earlier put in place. From January 1943 all women aged between 17 and 45 were required to register to work. This was extended later to women aged 50. By 1945, almost 60% of workers were women. Some became Trümmerfrauen, whose job it was to clear the 14 billion cubic feet of bricks and rubble left from Allied bombing.

> **Trümmerfrauen**
> Literally means 'rubble women' or 'ruins women'. They were employed to help demolish the remains of buildings and clear up the resulting debris.

The mass return of women to work would have had an impact on family life, which of course was also affected by the loss of millions of servicemen. German society was also left with a gender imbalance, with women outnumbering men.

The most significant changes in the nature and composition of society were in the main the consequence of:
- military service and losses at the front
- the destruction of industries and the dislocation of the workforce
- evacuation and homelessness.

An estimated 3.2 million civilians had been killed in the hostilities. In the region of 4 million flats and houses out of an original total of 17.1 million had been destroyed. In Düsseldorf alone, 9 out of 10 houses had been damaged. In Berlin 75% of all homes were rendered uninhabitable.

The aftermath of war

Following the defeat of the Third Reich, the Allied leaders were determined to put the Nazi ringleaders and those primarily responsible for unleashing the Second World War on trial. Twelve trials involving over 100 defendants took place in Nuremberg, regarded as the spiritual home of Nazism, between 1945 and 1949. The first trial took place on 20 November 1945 and involved the prosecution of 21 major Nazi criminals.

All other German people were to be denazified and German society cleansed of National Socialist ideology. However, some pro-Nazi sentiments persisted, with the result that many of those who had lived through the Third Reich became defensive about the extent of their participation in the Nazi state. Many German people resented the intrusive questioning about their past and many came to see themselves as victims of another victor's peace when confronted with the appalling crimes that had been committed in Hitler's name. In addition, the German people could also point to their own sufferings: loss of civilian life through Allied bombing, the mass rapes perpetrated by the Red Army as they advanced west, and the misery caused by food shortages and the destruction of homes, businesses and infrastructure.

Denazification involved a strategy to forbid important jobs to former Nazis in the rebuilding of post-war Germany. However, this proved impractical because it was almost impossible to find experts and engineers who were not in some way tainted by association with Nazism.

Summary

When you have completed this section, you should have a thorough knowledge of the impact of changing Nazi foreign policy in the period 1933–45.

- The extent to which Nazi foreign policy in the period 1933–45 revealed a continuity with the past, such as the revisionist policies of the Weimar Republic.
- The way in which Hitler manipulated international relations in the period 1933–39, such as the Non-Aggression Pact with Poland in 1934.
- The reasons why the Nazis were able to achieve their aims and objectives in foreign policy in the period 1933–39 including rearmament and Anschluss.
- The changing fortunes of the German military machine in the period 1939–45 such as the early Blitzkrieg successes and the difficulties on the Russian front.
- How the desire for race and space become the main driver for German foreign policy in the period 1933–45.
- The impact of total war on the German people such as the destruction caused by Allied bombing and the changing pace of war work.

Questions & Answers

This section includes a guide to the structure of the examination for the Depth Unit 4 Option 8 Germany: Democracy and Dictatorship c.1918–1945; Part 2: Nazi Germany c.1933–1945 in the WJEC specification. This is followed by an explanation of the assessment objectives and a guide to how best to allocate your time to fit the mark allocations. It is important that you familiarise yourself with the exam structure and the nature of the assessments. After each past paper question there are two exemplar answers. One represents an A grade (Student A) and the other a C grade (Student B). The strengths and weaknesses of each answer are included within the provided commentary.

The structure of the exam

There will be a compulsory source-based question in Section A of your exam paper. In Section B you are required to answer one of two open-ended essay questions. Each question will be marked out of 30. You will have 1 hour and 45 minutes to complete your answers.

The nature of the assessment objectives

Question 1 is entirely based on AO2. You are expected to 'analyse and evaluate appropriate source material, primary and/or contemporary to the period, within its historical context'.

Students are expected to:
- analyse and evaluate three sources in the context of their origin and in the context of the set enquiry
- assess the value of each of the three sources to a historian undertaking a specific enquiry
- show that they understand the historical context surrounding the enquiry and are able to offer some judgement on the value of the sources to a historian undertaking a specific enquiry.

Questions 2 and 3 (of which you pick one) are entirely based on AO1. You are expected to 'demonstrate, organise and communicate knowledge and understanding to analyse and evaluate the key features related to the periods studied, making substantiated judgements and exploring concepts, as relevant, of cause and consequence, change, continuity, similarity, difference and significance'.

Students are expected to:
- analyse and evaluate and reach a balanced and substantiated judgement on the key concept in the set question
- support their responses with selected and appropriate historical knowledge.

Questions 2 and 3 are not about providing a narrative of events and developments related to the question. You are expected to engage in a debate in relation to the key concept in the question and to reach a valid judgement.

Timing your answer

This guide suggests that you split your time evenly between each question.

■ Section A

Question 1

Study the sources below and answer the question that follows.

Source A

Wales and Germany have one grave problem in common — how to tackle unemployment. In Germany the fight has been carried on with energy. The German Government has encouraged a Voluntary Labour Service of public works, which has set up thousands of labour camps throughout Germany. The members of the camps are all volunteers. They work about six hours a day, some on roads, some in draining marshes, others in clearing the results of floods, some in building sports grounds. These young men do not work for profit, for they only receive pocket-money. They are given, however, plain but good food, work-clothes, exercise, health and comradeship, and work from four to nine months in the camp. All the work done is for the public good and not for the benefit of an individual. Indeed the Hitler Government wishes to make it compulsory and turn it into a kind of national conscription scheme. Perhaps by these labour camps Germany may be leading the way to a method of rescuing the youth of Europe from the effects of unemployment. The Trade Unions however, oppose the Voluntary Labour Service, which they see as a menace to the wage agreements they have struggled for.

Source A Gareth Jones, 'How Germany Tackles Unemployment', *Western Mail,* February 1933. The article was written following a visit to Germany.

Source B

Under the lash of dictatorship, the level of economic activity has been greatly increased. The exploitation of labour has been greatly increased by the abolition of the 8 hour day, which has been gained over generations, and by the extraordinary increase in work rate. A fascist system which makes marriage and the procreation of as many children as possible the highest duty of a subject, cannot afford in the long run continually to reduce housing capacity for the expanding and increasing number of households. 12–13 billions of Reich marks are squeezed from the national income for rearmament, but even then one cannot do everything at once with the extorted billions. One cannot simultaneously increase armaments for land and air, build up a massive fleet, build gigantic installations and construct grandiose buildings. On the basis of the living standards of the German people hitherto, one can either do one or the other or a bit of everything, but not everything at the same time and in unlimited dimensions.

Source B A secret report for the leadership of the German Social Democratic Party in exile (SOPADE). The report assesses the economic situation in Germany in July 1938 and was circulated abroad.

Source C

We face a serious military challenge in Russia. Total war is the demand of the hour. The danger facing us is enormous. The efforts we take to meet it must be just as enormous. We can no longer make only partial and careless use of the war potential at home and in the significant parts of Europe that we control. We must use our full resources, as quickly and thoroughly as it is organisationally and practically possible. We are voluntarily giving up a significant part of our living standard to increase our war effort as quickly and completely as possible. This is not an end in itself, but rather a means to an end. The total war effort has become a matter of the entire German people. No one has any excuse for ignoring its demands. We must bear any burden, even the heaviest, to make any sacrifice, if it leads to the great goal of victory. Everyone must learn to pay heed to war morale, and pay attention to the just demands of working and fighting people. The problem is freeing soldiers for the front, and

freeing workers for the armaments industry. The reason for our current measures is to mobilise the necessary workers. The duty for women to work is vital. The more who join the war effort, the more soldiers we can free for the front. I am convinced that the German woman is determined to fill the spot left by the man leaving for the front, and to do so as soon as possible.

Source C Joseph Goebbels, minister of propaganda, in a radio broadcast to the German people entitled 'Nation Rise Up, And Let the Storm Break Loose', Berlin, 1943.

With reference to the sources and your understanding of the historical context, assess the value of these three sources to a historian studying Nazi economic policy between 1933 and 1943.

[30 marks]

Student A

These sources are valuable to a historian studying the development of Nazi economic policy in the period 1933–43 as they cover all three phases of Nazi economic development, namely, the recovery in 1933, rearmament from 1936–38 and total war in the period after 1943 under Albert Speer.

Source A was written by a visiting foreign journalist and shows the methods that the Nazis were using to rebuild the shattered German economy following the Wall Street Crash of 1929. The resulting economic depression had caused a huge unemployment problem within Germany of up to 6 million people.

The Weimar Republic began a programme of public works which was continued by the Nazis, only they had seemingly made it more effective. This source is valuable to a historian because it shows the starting point for the redevelopment of the economy under the Nazis under Schacht who was the initiator of the German recovery. Of course, this was all tied into the consolidation of power because the Nazis saw a successful economic policy as a means of winning support.

In fact, the article ignores some of the most negative aspects of the Nazi programme, which removed women and Jewish people from the economy.

Also, it is clear to a historian, however, that not everyone had been won over by this programme, because the Trade Unions were opposed. Later they would be abolished. The tone of the source is largely positive because the reporter, who is from Wales, is comparing what is going on in Wales at the same time, and he sees the government action taken in Germany as a positive step.

He may have been swayed by the fact that at this point there was some international support for the regime, especially since it would be a strong state in Europe that would prevent the threat of communism.

The fact that this is a newspaper article may affect the veracity of the source to a historian studying economic policy, because the article seems to take at face value what the Nazis were attempting to do and offers it as a possible solution to what was happening in Britain at the same time. It could be possible that the author was too sympathetic to the Nazi economic programme.

ⓔ The student has attempted an analysis and evaluation of Source A and not simply summarised the content of the source. The source evaluation comments are developed, and the student has attempted to place the source within the general context of the set enquiry. There are references to the Depression and unemployment. The student has provided a judgement on the value of the source to a historian studying Nazi economic policy in the period 1933–43.

Source B is from a report from the exiled Social Democratic Party. It is commenting upon the effects of the Four-Year Plan, which was introduced by Goering in 1936. The plan set Germany on a course for vigorous rearmament at all costs. The tone of the source is obviously anti-Nazi given that it is from the political opposition, and so a historian would have to treat the source with caution.

The source is valuable to a historian studying economic policy because it gives a contemporary viewpoint of the developments in Nazi economic policy and shows how rearmament was the economic priority of the regime despite the social consequences. However, it is true to say that Hitler did not want to lose the support of the people by making the domestic situation impossible for them, even though Goering had coined the phrase 'guns or butter'.

The source is valuable to a historian because it shows that the Nazi regime was driven by its ideological goals for foreign policy and that it did not always make the right choices. Rearmament was the first step on the road to an aggressive foreign policy.

ⓔ The student has again avoided simply extracting information from within the source. There is some good contextual awareness although the student drifts into a general discussion of the significance of Nazi economic policy. The student has produced some meaningful source evaluation which reflects the general context of the source. Although the student has focused on the development of economic policy, he/she needed to focus on more date-specific historical context in order to produce a more reasoned judgement on the value of the source to a historian.

Source C is a radio broadcast by the propaganda minister Joseph Goebbels. In this broadcast, Goebbels is trying to motivate the German people towards a commitment to total war. The economic demands of war were great, and he is calling upon all German people to step up to the challenge.

The source is valuable to a historian studying economic policy because it shows how a social policy of keeping women out of the workplace had now turned into an economic policy of necessity. It was a case of all hands on deck during the war.

The fact that Goebbels is the propaganda minister means that a historian will need to use this source carefully so that it might not be completely valuable to him/her.

However, there is a tone of desperation within this source that is valuable to a historian in showing that the war on two fronts, in the west and the east, was taking its toll on the German people and that the war economy was not meeting the military needs.

Overall, the three sources are valuable to a historian because they show how Nazi economic policy had developed in the period 1933–43 and how the economic priorities had changed. The sources show that in 1933 the issue was an all-out attack on unemployment, which would enable the Nazis to consolidate the regime. The second source shows how the Nazis were now on an ideological mission to rearm so that they could pursue the aggressive policies shown in Source C.

ℯ The student did not take the chance to consider the context of 1943 and this means that there has been an imbalance in the treatment of the three sources in the response. The source evaluation comments are a little more mechanistic and formulaic in relation to Source C. The student needed to place the source in the context of the events of 1943 that led to the radio broadcast. In this way the context of the origin of the source can be directly linked to the subject of economic policy.

Overall the student has attempted to analyse and evaluate all three sources in relation to some specific and some general context of the set enquiry. A sound judgement is seen regarding the value of the sources to a historian in at least two out of the three sources.

ℯ Score: 23/30 marks = A*/A borderline

Student B

Between 1933 and 1943 the Nazi economy went through a number of different developments. The three sources show a number of different stages in the development.

Source A is from a newspaper article written in the Western Mail. The source focuses on how Germany was tackling unemployment in 1933. The source tells us that the Nazi government is continuing with a Voluntary Labour Service of public works, which set up thousands of labour camps throughout Germany. All the work was done for the public good. The source says that the Nazis wanted to make the scheme compulsory, but the German Trade Unions were opposed to such a scheme.

The source is from February 1933, which is one month after the Nazis came to power in Germany and one month before the March 5th election, which resulted in the Nazis consolidating their power inside Germany.

This is useful to a historian as it was produced outside of Germany by a visiting reporter. The reporter will have witnessed what he saw although he may have exaggerated what he said because reporters tend to sensationalise just to sell newspapers.

e The student has extracted information from the first source and made some very mechanistic source evaluation comments about the type of source. The student has also failed to focus on the correct historical context — they have looked at the context in relation to Nazi consolidation of power rather than economic policy. The student has incorrectly provided a mechanistic judgement on the utility of the source rather than on the value of the source to a historian studying economic policy in the period 1933–43.

> Source B is from a secret report from the German Social Democratic Party and was produced in July 1938. During this time the party would spy on events inside Germany and spread its findings throughout Europe. This could be biased because the party would say negative things about the Nazi regime because it was in exile. This source is also useful for a historian studying Nazi economic policy because it is from the point of view of the opposition.
>
> The source shows that Germany is rearming at this time and that it was having a negative effect on the standard of living of the German people. The government was spending between 12 and 13 billion Reich marks on rearmament.
>
> The tone of this source is very negative, and this would be very useful to a historian studying Nazi economic policy because it is not a piece of Nazi propaganda but is telling the historian what they saw in Germany in 1938.

e The student has continued to focus on the content of the source, extracting some information from it about rearmament. There is also mechanistic source evaluation which focuses upon tone and bias. Once again, the student has failed to bring any contextual awareness either general or appropriate to the answer about Nazi economic policy in 1938. The judgement is again focusing on the utility of the source and fails to answer the precise question set.

> Finally, Source C is from a radio broadcast by Joseph Goebbels who was Germany's propaganda minister. This will obviously be biased because he will present the Nazis and their policies in a positive light. The source tells a historian that Germany was now operating a total war economy and that all of society was geared to the war effort. It shows that women were now working full out in the factories and that allowed more men to be used at the front line. This is useful to a historian because it shows them that the main focus of the economy was for war.
>
> In conclusion all the sources are useful to a historian studying Nazi economic policy between 1933 and 1943. Source A is the least useful as it talks mainly about Weimar economic policy. Source B was very useful because it shows a change to rearmament, but it is very biased because it shows the attitude of a disgruntled political party in exile. Source C is also very useful because it shows the focus on total war.

(e) Source C follows a similar pattern to the other two sources. The response is constructed around what the student had been given within the provided materials. The student has not brought anything additional in terms of the context of each source or the context of the precise question on economic policy. It is largely a source-based response with some mechanistic evaluation that focuses on the types of source.

The response attempts to consider the content of the provided material and offers a limited judgement on the utility of each of the three sources to a historian studying Nazi economic policy. The student has considered the relative value of the sources in the conclusion, but this is not required by the specific demands of the question.

(e) **Score: 15/30 marks = C/D borderline**

■ Section B

Answer ONE question, either Question 2 or Question 3.

Question 2

How effective were social, religious and racial policies in maintaining support for the Nazi regime in the period 1933–1945?

> **Student A**
>
> It could be argued that the social, religious and racial policies were effective in maintaining support for the Nazi regime although they led to changing levels of support for the Nazi regime at different times and to different degrees. For example, the Concordat of 1933 ensured the immediate compliance of the Catholic church, but it did not stop the church criticising the euthanasia programme in 1937. Whilst the banning of trade unions in 1933 may have effectively silenced the voice of the working classes, it did not prevent unofficial strikes and go-slows over poor pay and long hours.

🅔 The student has engaged with the precise question set and begins with a thoughtful overall analysis and evaluation of the effectiveness of social, religious and racial policies in maintaining support for the Nazi regime between 1933 and 1945. The introduction should allow the student to enter into a debate on the key concept rather than produce a generalised list of social, religious and racial policies.

> The social policies of the Nazis resulted in changing levels of support but were mainly effective in maintaining support for the Nazi regime. The youth policy for example was initially very successful in attracting the support of young people and German people in general. Young people were indoctrinated into becoming loyal Nazis although Sopade reports challenge this general support by suggesting that young people were more supportive of the organisation itself rather than the Nazi Party which had implemented it. The young people were thirsting for action and were rebellious by nature. However, despite the widespread initial support there developed a separate Swing Youth culture as the Hitler Youth became more military based and many young people turned to church organisations.
>
> Women also shifted their support to and from the regime as a result of Nazi social policy. Women were initially forced out of work, as the Nazis saw the role of women differently in terms of a natural domestic role as wives and mothers. Child bonuses and loans for families were offered to German women. However, those women who were squeezed out of the professions, and who were forced back into work because rearmament and conscription created a labour shortage, suffered from the burdens of long hours and family responsibilities.
>
> Some women relished their new status and willingly surrendered their political freedoms and working opportunities for the status that Nazism gave them. They openly collaborated with the spreading of Nazi values. Overall, women complied with the expectations of Nazi social policy, and so in this respect they were very effective.

Propaganda and indoctrination were used throughout society in order to create a malleable population. The Nazis were keen on creating a National Community through their social policies and most German people were keen to become part of this idealised community.

e The student has started to debate the key concept in the question in relation to social policy. The approach remains largely analytical and a judgement has been reached in relation to the effectiveness of Nazi social policy in maintaining support for the Nazi regime.

The Nazi religious policies were never really fully effective in maintaining support. The support for the church was too strong. The Concordat had initially won the support of the church because it had agreed to restrict itself to religious issues and not comment upon political matters. However, the Pope was critical of the fact that the Nazi regime did not stick to the terms of the Concordat of 1933. The church became distrustful of the Nazi regime. The idea of creating a Nazi Reich church was not supported and indeed the Confessional church was established in opposition. Bishop Galen of the Catholic church also publicly criticised the euthanasia programme.

Nazi racial policy was met with little resistance and so must have been effective in maintaining support, because anti-Semitism was widespread throughout Europe even before the Nazis came to power. Jewish people were targeted firstly with the boycotting of businesses. The Nuremberg Laws followed in 1935, which deprived Jewish people of citizenship. Concentration camps were established later in the move towards the Final Solution.

There was some opposition to anti-Semitism but there few examples of public opposition to the policy. Therefore, it could be said that racial policies were effective in maintaining support for the regime. For example, the idea of a master race was not opposed by most people.

e The student has focused on some aspects of religious and racial policy although there has been a tendency to drift towards explanation in places rather than focusing on developing a debate through analysis and evaluation of the key issues. There needs to be a more meaningful and reasoned evaluation of the key issues. There is an attempt to come to some sort of balanced judgement on religious and racial policy in relation to the question.

To conclude, social, religious and racial policies were at times both effective and ineffective in maintaining support for the Nazi regime. Initially it is probably true to say that the policies were effective because the church was at first content with the fact that their institutions were protected, and the Nazis had destroyed communism. The early racial policies were accepted although there was some opposition to how far it developed, especially during the war. Social policies were met with little or no opposition. It is probably true that most German people lived in fear of Nazi terror and so that would have made social, religious and racial policies appear more effective than perhaps they actually were.

ⓔ The response is mainly focused on debating the key concept in the set question. The response deals with a number of the main developments although the quality of the debate varies at times. There is a reasonably balanced and appropriate judgement. The student has made a successful attempt overall at dealing with the key issues and answering the precise question set.

ⓔ **Score: 23/30 marks = A*/A borderline**

Question 3

How far do you agree that Hitler's leadership was mainly responsible for Germany's defeat in the Second World War?

> **Student B**
>
> There are many contributing factors as to why Germany lost the Second World War. These include key military defeats like the invasion of Stalingrad and the fact that the German economy was unprepared for a prolonged war. Also included here should be the strength of the Allied forces and finally Hitler's weak leadership. I will consider each of these issues in turn and reach an overall judgement on why Germany was defeated.

ⓔ The student has not engaged with the precise question set. The student has failed to identify the key concept in the question in this case, whether Hitler was mainly responsible for Germany's defeat in the Second World War. The student has set out a list of contributing factors to Germany's defeat, and the danger is that the response will revolve around a generalised discussion of these factors, events and developments.

> When Germany invaded Poland in 1939, Germany was not really prepared for a major war. Goering's Four-Year Plan was designed to create a war economy, but throughout the later stages of the war, the economy greatly suffered. The primary reason for the failure of the economy was that precedence was given to ideological aims, which took precedence over military need. For example, the railways were used to transport Jewish people to the concentration camps rather than transporting materials to factories and the front line. This affected the German army and had a long-term impact on the effectiveness of their military campaign.
>
> As a result, the German army was unable to combat the effects of the Russian winters following the invasion in 1941. This eventually contributed towards the defeat at Stalingrad, which was a major turning point in the failure of German military success. Also, the persecution of the Jewish people had an enormous negative impact on Germany's potential to win the war, because the removal of Jewish scientists from weapons developments denied the German army

access to nuclear weapons, which could have altered the outcome of the war. Also, industry in Germany could not compete with the might and power of both America and the Soviet Union. So, the economy had a great effect upon Germany's defeat.

ⓔ The student has discussed the economic reasons for Germany's defeat but has made no attempt to link this to the issue of Hitler's leadership. There is a hint that the student is beginning to focus upon turning points during the war rather than focusing on the precise question set.

It could also be argued that the alliance of Britain, America and the Soviet Union was detrimental to Germany. Events such as D-Day played a role in Germany's defeat. This was a well-planned operation which convinced the Germans that the attack would come from Calais and not Normandy.

Operation Overlord was arguably the greatest turning point during the war. Also, the failure of Operation Barbarossa was a decisive factor in the defeat of Germany because it led to the creation of a two-front war. Germany was forced to split its resources in order to meet the challenges of both war in the east and the west. The initial aim was to capture the Caucasus oil fields, which would have given Germany access to vital resources.

The focus on Stalingrad had no real benefit to the German war effort other than satisfying an ideological obsession by the Nazi regime to defeat Bolshevism. The German defeat at Stalingrad was another turning point in the war.

ⓔ The student has continued to identify turning points in the Second World War. There is the beginning of a move towards the leadership issue with the reference to the invasion being an ideological obsession, but this is not developed in any way. Overall there is a considerable drift away from the precise question set.

There is no doubt that Hitler made some very questionable military decisions. He certainly made a mistake in invading the Soviet Union, but probably one of his greatest mistakes was not to take advantage of the trapped Allied troops at Dunkirk. Also, he refocused German bombing raids towards the cities and away from the bases. In this way, Hitler's poor leadership was another reason for Germany's military defeat in the Second World War.

ⓔ Here is the first real reference to Hitler's leadership but only in terms of his military strategy. Furthermore, the focus on leadership is presented as yet another factor in the subsequent defeat of Germany. There is no attempt to weigh up the significance of leadership against the other factors to reach a judgement on what was mainly responsible for Germany's defeat. The focus is still upon a general response to what combination of factors was responsible.

To conclude, there were several reasons why Germany was defeated during the Second World War and Hitler's leadership was clearly one of those reasons. The weaknesses of the economy, events such as D-Day and Italy's surrender had an effect. Hitler's decision to invade the Soviet Union also had an effect, because he created a two-front war and they were fighting against the world's strongest powers. Although Germany suffered many military losses at the hands of the Allies, it is likely that had it not been for Hitler's poor leadership qualities, Germany potentially would have had a far greater chance of winning the war.

Therefore, overall, I believe that Hitler's leadership was mainly responsible for Germany's defeat.

e The response has some focus on the key issues and begins to discuss these to come to a judgement on the question set. A limited but valid judgement has been reached but it is not reasoned or fully supported elsewhere within the answer. The issue of Hitler's leadership being mainly responsible for the defeat of Germany has not been addressed and so the key concept in the question has not been debated. The first direct reference to the key concept appears at the end of the answer. A number of assertions have been made within the response, but they have not been supported. This response lacks analysis and evaluation of the key concept.

e Score: 15/30 marks = C/D borderline

Knowledge check answers

1 The Wall Street Crash radicalised political opinion inside Germany as economic hardship or the fear of it led to massive growth in support for the Nazis. The Nazi Party was openly hostile to the Republic. Hitler offered strong leadership and promised to eradicate the threat from growing support for the KPD.

2 Support for the KPD increased from 590,000 votes in June 1920 and 4 seats in the Reichstag, to 5,980,000 votes in November 1932 and 100 seats in the Reichstag.

3 Göring encouraged the use of violence when dealing with acts of terrorism by Communists. In fact, he basically set the tone that it was a public duty to shoot Communists. This decree in itself shows the inability of Papen to control Göring.

4 Although the Communists were blamed for the Reichstag Fire, there is an argument that the Nazis were responsible because they wanted to discredit the Communists and create an atmosphere of 'Red Peril'. Others have concluded that it was the work of Van der Lubbe, a Dutch anarchist, acting independently.

5 The Nazis calculated that allowing the KPD to contest the election would be a prudent move, because the traditional animosity between the SPD and the KPD was likely to resurface and once again split the socialist vote. It would give the Nazis a better chance of gaining an overall majority.

6 Röhm argued that the political revolution had been achieved but he also wanted the destruction of the remaining reactionary forces, including the army in its existing form, and a move towards greater social mobility within society.

7 The Winter Help campaign encouraged Germans to have a one-pot meal, an Eintopf, once a week. The money saved went into collections to alleviate the suffering of the poor.

8 Claus von Stauffenberg was horrified by the war-time carnage he witnessed in Russia and the treatment of Slavic civilians. In the context of the defeat at Stalingrad and the D-Day landings he felt that the war's continuation would lead to a waste of human life. He therefore felt impelled to act against Hitler.

9 Anti-Semitic propaganda was delivered to the German people through Nazi newspapers such as *Der Stürmer* and publications such as *Mein Kampf*, and also through speeches, propaganda posters, education and organisations such as the Hitler Youth. It was put into practice in discriminatory legislation and violence carried out by the SA and SS.

10 The president and the foreign minister opposed the boycott of Jewish businesses. They had concerns about the negative impact on the economy. There was a negative reaction to events in the foreign press. The general public were largely apathetic and some ignored the boycott.

11 A series of discriminatory laws was passed in 1933.
   - On 28 March 1933 Hitler proclaimed a general boycott of Jewish people which was issued to all Nazi Party organisations.
   - On 1 April there was a boycott of Jewish businesses.
   - On 7 April the Law for the Restoration of the Professional Civil Service officially excluded Jewish people from working in the civil service.
   - On 25 April a law against the overcrowding of German schools limited the number of places for Jewish children.
   - A law passed on 6 May prevented Jewish people being employed as lecturers, and another on 2 June stopped them working as dentists.
   - From 28 September non-Aryans and anyone married to a non-Aryan were excluded from all government posts.
   - On 29 September Jewish people were banned from all cultural and entertainment activities.
   - In early October the National Press Law prevented Jewish people from working in the press.

12 Mixed marriages were forbidden under the terms of the Law for the Protection of German Blood and Honour. Also, by this law, German women under the age of 45 could no longer be employed in Jewish households. The Reich Citizenship Law reduced German Jewish people to a second-class status.

13 The Cross of Honour of the German Mother, or Mutterkreuz (Mother's Cross) for short, was introduced in 1939 and awarded to mothers who had given birth to a certain number of children. A bronze medal was given to those with four, silver for six and gold for eight. For the mother to be eligible, she and her husband had to be of German blood, and the children free from any hereditary illnesses or disorders.

14 All citizens should have a decent life and a job. All citizens should have equal rights and obligations. The first duty of a citizen is to work, either physically or mentally. Personal enrichment by means of war is a crime against the nation. All public owned companies should be nationalised.

15 The Nazis invested a billion marks in Arbeitsdienst (public works). There was a programme of road, canal and house building, together with afforestation, land reclamation and motorisation.

16 Industrialists gained more from the economic recovery than the middle classes or the workers. Although some industrialists resented state control, they benefited from the expansion of the economy and the smashing of the trade unions. Small businesses gained from the economic recovery, but they could not compete with big business, and small farmers did not prosper. For workers the picture is mixed because some skilled personnel did well. Generally, the workers gained jobs but lost their rights to free collective bargaining. Their hours of work tended to be longer.

17 Continuous thread: the Kaiserreich promoted colonisation and the Pan-German League had its own expansionist doctrine. Gustav Stresemann in the Weimar period wanted the revision of the terms of the Treaty of Versailles, protection of German people abroad and the readjustment of the eastern frontier. This continuous thread in foreign policy built a bridge to the revisionism of the early 1930s and a platform for the Nazi pursuit of Lebensraum after 1939.

18 The German government made various tactical agreements between 1934 and 1939.

- A Non-Aggression Pact was signed with Poland in January 1934 following the German withdrawal from the League of Nations. This bilateral agreement interfered with France's alliance with Poland and also allayed the West's suspicions about Germany's designs on Poland.
- In March 1935, Hitler announced the existence of a German air force and on 16 March he introduced conscription. A favourable naval agreement was signed with Britain to offset German rearmament.
- In 1936, an Axis agreement was reached with Italy, which recognised mutual spheres of interest, and an Anti-Comintern Pact was signed with Japan against communism.
- In May 1939, the Pact of Steel was agreed with Italy and in August 1939 Germany signed a Non-Aqgression Pact with Russia, as a temporary expedient to avoid a two-front war.

19 The Hossbach Memorandum was an unofficial record of a meeting at the Berlin Reich chancellery on 5 November 1937. With this document, Hitler outlined his foreign policy aims and methods. According to the minutes of the meeting taken by Colonel Hossbach (Hitler's military adjutant), the tempo of Hitler's diplomacy had changed. He was now prepared to take more risks and to use force. The expansionism of German foreign policy, which had remained latent, now became explicit.

20 Hitler had exploited the unwillingness of Britain and France to take direct action in support of Czechoslovakia, so that German aggression had been rewarded. The agreement signed at Munich provided for the German occupation of Sudetenland, and the assimilation of its 3.5 million German minority into the Reich. Munich revealed much about the nature of international relations, because the crisis had been resolved by Italy, Germany, Britain and France, and they had forced their decision upon Czechoslovakia. Russia had not been consulted and became isolated from the West. Yet some see Munich as a failure for Hitler because he had allowed himself to be talked into a diplomatic agreement instead of pursuing the military solution, which he had threatened to use throughout the crisis.

21 The Locarno spirit was a symbol of reconciliation and cooperation which created an illusion that real peace had come at last through the Locarno agreements of 1925. Gustav Stresemann was prepared to make concessions that would return Germany to full sovereignty and independence in the future. However, Locarno did not remove the aims of eliminating reparations, achieving military equality or revising Germany's eastern frontiers.

Index